Artwork and Additional Texts

for Common Worship

Compiled by Sarah Roberts
Illustrated by Melody-Anne Lee

kevin
mayhew

Important Copyright Information

First published in 2008 by
KEVIN MAYHEW LTD
Buxhall, Stowmarket, Suffolk, IP14 3BW
E-mail: info@kevinmayhewltd.com
www.kevinmayhew.com

9 8 7 6 5 4 3 2 1 0

ISBN 978 1 84417 950 3
Catalogue No. 1501080

Illustrated by Melody-Anne Lee
Cover design by Melody-Anne Lee
Edited by Sarah Roberts
Typesetting by Richard Weaver

Printed and bound in Great Britain

Contents

ORDINARY TIME

Foreword

This book is intended for anyone involved in preparing service sheets, newsletters and worship based on the Common Worship Lectionary.

For every week of the three-year cycle there is

> **an original and vibrant drawing by Melody-Anne Lee illustrating an aspect of the Readings.**

There are also one or more of the following, each developing and encapsulating the Sunday or Feast Day theme

> **a prayer or intercession**
>
> **a poem**
>
> **a metrical, easily sung, psalm of the day**
>
> **a hymn to a well-known tune which draws together the themes of the readings.**

Much of the material is suitable for all-age worship.

Purchasers of this book may download or photocopy the material for use in service sheets and newsletters. The use of psalms and hymns should be reported on CCLI returns.

If you are not a member of CCLI please contact the publisher direct for permission.

ADVENT

Advent 1

Year A

Isaiah 2:1-5
Psalm 122
Romans 13:11-14
Matthew 24:36-44

They shall beat their swords into ploughshares, and their spears into pruning-hooks.
(Isaiah 2:4b)

Prayer

Eternal Father, we thank you for this Advent season of hope and expectation.
We thank you that, even in these dark days of approaching winter,
we can celebrate the coming of the light.

O Lord of light and truth:
Shine in our darkness.

We thank you for the life of Jesus Christ, and the light of goodness which he brought into the world. We thank you that his light has inspired prophets and saints in every generation to overcome the darkness of hate, fear, greed, lust and callous indifference with the radiance of love, faith, generosity, kindness and compassion. May that same radiance enlighten this present age.

O Lord of light and truth:
Shine in our darkness.

We thank you for the Gospel of Jesus Christ, which gives hope of the coming of your Kingdom. Give the light of hope to those who live in the darkness of conflict, poverty and oppression. Give the light of hope to those who labour for peace, justice and human dignity.

O Lord of light and truth:
Shine in our darkness.

We thank you for the Spirit of Jesus Christ, which shines wherever there is compassion, forgiveness and healing. Holy Spirit, shine even in our lives, to bring comfort to those who mourn, release to those who are burdened with anxiety or guilt, friendship to those who are lonely, strength to the sick and peace to those who live in fear.

O Lord of light and truth:
Shine in our darkness.

Lord, give us grace in this Advent season to cast aside the works of darkness and put on the armour of light, for the sake of Jesus Christ our Lord. Amen.

Peter Dainty

Hymn

The King is coming soon to reign
in splendid resurrection power –
although we cannot name the hour
we know he soon will come again.

Let all take note, and not forget
that there will be a judgement day;
God's mercy lengthens its delay –
his patience has not ended yet.

That day will bring both gain and loss
as each receives a just reward:
for saints, the welcome of their Lord,
but shame for all who spurned his cross.

Though now we taste mortality,
his glorious promise we believe:
when Jesus comes, we shall receive
new bodies for eternity.

Till then he tells us: watch and pray
and in his service labour on;
our time on earth will soon be gone –
for he may well return today!

Martin E. Leckebusch

Metre: 8 88 8 (LM)
Suggested tunes: *Winchester New; Church Triumphant*

Advent 1

Year B

Isaiah 64:1-9
Psalm 80:1-8, 18-20
1 Corinthians 1:3-9
Mark 13:24-37

Restore us, O Lord God of hosts; let your face shine, that we may be saved.
(Psalm 80:19)

Prayer

Lord Jesus Christ,
just as you walked and talked on our earth,
present among your people,
sharing our humanity,
ministering your love,
living and dying alongside us,
teach us that you are here now through your Spirit,
equally as near and involved,
just as eager to show your love
and minister your grace.
Grant now, as we come together in your name,
that we might sense your presence,
hear your voice
and learn more of your redeeming, renewing power,
so that we will be open to all you would do
among us
and equipped to live more faithfully as your people,
to your glory.
Amen.

Nick Fawcett

Psalm 80

Shepherd of the chosen flock,
mighty One, enthroned on high,
God whom angel hosts adore,
hear our humble, ardent cry:
let your glory flood our sight!
Rise in holy, saving might:

Show your face in mercy, Lord –
may your people be restored.

How long will your anger blaze?
How long will you spurn our prayer?
How long must our bitter tears
bring a foretaste of despair?
From our neighbours we have bore
cruel contempt and brazen scorn:

Once you cleared a plot of land,
planting there a tender vine;
there it spread its leafy boughs,
there its fruit was lush and fine.
Now that fruit, abandoned, falls;
broken are the vineyard walls:

Recognise our deep distress:
Lord, your vine is now laid waste;
see the saints whom once you chose
now, at your rebuke, disgraced.
Let your call again be known,
claim your servants as your own:

Martin E. Leckebusch

Metre: 77 77 77 refrain 77
Suggested tune: *St George's Windsor*

Advent 1

Year C

Jeremiah 33:14-16
Psalm 25:1-9
1 Thessalonians 3:9-13
Luke 21:25-36

Make me to know your ways, O Lord; teach me your paths. (Psalm 25:4)

Psalm 25

Lord, I gladly trust in you:
let me not be put to shame.
As I look towards your throne
make your gracious promise known:
God my refuge and my hope,
your protective care I claim.

In your hands I place my past:
all my sins you know so well.
Your forgiveness, Lord, I need,
for my guilt is great indeed;
even greater is your love –
mercy more than I can tell.

Teach me what is true and good;
let me hear and understand!
In the choices I must make
show my heart the way to take,
so that I may always tread
on the path which you have planned.

When my troubles multiply
you alone can bring me through:
so with all your saints I say,
'Be my strength and shield today.'
Since I know you hear my prayer,
Lord, I gladly trust in you.

Martin E. Leckebusch

Metre: 77 77 77
Suggested tunes: *Petra; Ratisbon*

Poem

Somewhere between the ornaments
and the electric toys,
The Child was lost.
Perhaps it was the noise,
perhaps the cost
of Christmas gifts these days,
perhaps the maze of counters
and the gaze
of faces lost to love
beneath the glaze of weariness.

He was right next to me for a while.
I remember his sweetness, his smile.
Perhaps I turned up the wrong aisle.
I am, I suppose, looking for Bethlehem
here on the second floor.
Is this the place to look?
Or will the clerk be telling me
that they don't carry holy mystery
in this department any more?

Elizabeth Rooney

Advent 2

Year A

Isaiah 11:1-10
Psalm 72:1-7, 18, 19
Romans 15:4-13
Matthew 3:1-12

His winnowing-fork is in his hand, and he will clear his threshing-floor and will gather his wheat into the granary; but the chaff he will burn with unquenchable fire. (Matthew 3:12)

Prayer

Father God,
just as you sent your servant John into the wilderness
to prepare the way of the Lord
and make ready your people to receive him,
so prepare us now to respond afresh to the gift of Christ
and to all that you offer us through him.
Give us a readiness truly to listen, learn, worship and respond,
receiving the forgiveness he extends
and the renewal he makes possible,
and giving back in return our heartfelt gratitude
expressed in true commitment and faithful service.
In his name we pray.
Amen.

Nick Fawcett

Poem

My sin, however great,
still cannot be
greater than God's forgiveness.
There will,
I think there almost must be,
pain –
the pain of knowing
how I've wounded Love.
And there must be
a turning back to him.
Facing what I have done,
what I've become,
and seeing as he sees.

But, oh, then comes
the sinking to my knees
in joy and praise
that Love can love me still,
can love and always has,
and always will.

Elizabeth Rooney

Advent 2

Year B

Isaiah 40:1-11
Psalm 85:1, 2, 8-13
2 Peter 3:8-15a
Mark 1:1-8

In the wilderness prepare the way of the Lord, make straight in the desert a highway for our God. (Isaiah 40:3)

Psalm 85

Your favour rested on this land
and brought your people mercy, Lord:
the richness of your grace was seen
in countless broken lives restored –
for holy wrath was held at bay
while sin and guilt were swept away.

But your rebuke now weighs us down:
will you be angry evermore?
Deliver us from all our sin,
revive us as you did before;
in your unfailing love renew
the joy your people find in you.

With ears attentive to your voice
and spirits hushed in reverent fear
we come to seek your saving touch,
the word of peace we need to hear:
as we renounce our foolish past,
Lord, make your glory known at last.

May righteousness and peace unite
and justice yield to tenderness;
may loyal hearts be our response
to heaven's gift of holiness –
Lord, fill our lives and flood our land
with all your gracious love has planned.

Martin E. Leckebusch

Metre: 88 88 88
Suggested tune: *Melita*

Poem

Isn't it time for someone
to shout in the desert
like wild John;
to come out from hiding
in those stone cold cathedrals
and mahogany chapels,
to climb down
from those polished pulpits,
and leave those pre-conditioned
packaged congregations?

Isn't it time for someone
to go out and shout in the desert
like wild John;
someone not dressed up
in man-made fibres,
or driving a limousine,
living on super-bread,
or sleeping on Slumberland,
or receiving ecclesiastical commission;
but someone like wild John,
with a wilderness diet,
and dressed for the desert;
apart from it all,
where he can see it straight?

Isn't it time for someone
to shout loud in the desert
like wild John;
washing the dust off our civilisation,
before the fire comes
and burns up the chaff;
cleansing the dirt
from a sordid generation
in a river of hope,
and bathing the wounds
of the violent centuries,
ready for healing?

Isn't it time for someone
to shout in the desert
like wild John:
'Level off the unjust hills;
fill in the oppressed valleys;
straighten the crooked ways
and make a smooth road
for the Lord to enter his Kingdom'?

Peter Dainty

Advent 2

Year C

Malachi 3:1-4
Canticle: Luke 1:68-79
Philippians 1:3-11
Luke 3:1-6

He will sit as a refiner and purifier of silver. (Malachi 3:3)

Prayer

Lord Jesus Christ,
prepare your way in our hearts
and make us ready to worship you.
Through our praying, thinking, singing and reading
cleanse our thoughts,
kindle our faith,
renew our commitment
and increase our love,
preparing your way in our lives,
so that we might be ready to love you faithfully
and serve you more effectively,
to the glory of your name.
Amen.

Nick Fawcett

Poem

I've failed to love you, Father,
as much as you love me,
content to offer, rather,
a feeble travesty,
a going through the motions,
a playing of the part;
too often my devotions
not springing from the heart.
I truly mean to follow,
but other voices call;
discipleship proves hollow
as yet again I fall.
Commitment proves expensive,
temptations lead astray,
demands prove too extensive,
self-interest wins the day,
Lord, hear my supplications,
have mercy and forgive;
see past the limitations
that scar the love I give.
Remould, renew, refashion,
that I might learn your way,
responding with the passion
you show to me each day.

Nick Fawcett

Advent 3

Year A

Isaiah 35:1-10
Psalm 146:5-10
or *Canticle:* Magnificat
James 5:7-10
Matthew 11:2-11

For waters shall break forth in the wilderness, and streams in the desert. (Isaiah 35:6b)

Prayer

Blessed are you, Lord our God,
who has promised us your salvation
through the prophets,
and that in you we will find healing and peace.
We come to you,
for in our coming we turn away from the darkness
and enter into the light of your presence and
your love.

Mighty God and Saviour,
we pray for your Church throughout the world,
that it may witness to you
not only in word but also in deed.
May the Church reflect your love for the world
and show your acceptance and forgiveness
for all peoples.

Come, Lord,
for our hope is in you.
Amen.

David Adam

Psalm 146

With resounding alleluias,
all through life my soul shall raise
one unending song of worship,
one unceasing hymn of praise,
celebrating God Eternal,
Lord of everlasting days.

Even this world's noblest rulers –
rich or powerful, strong or brave –
will not give the help they promise
from the confines of the grave;
Jacob's God, our Hope, our Helper –
he alone is sure to save.

Praise the Lord, who formed the heaven,
shaped the land and filled the sea;
praise the Lord, whose heart for justice
treats the poor with equity;
praise the Lord for blind eyes opened,
praise for captive souls set free.

Sing to God, who thwarts the wicked,
gives the hungry food to share,
guards and guides the frightened stranger,
lifts the downcast from despair;
he upholds the weak and lonely –
praise him for such tender care!

With resounding alleluias,
all through life my soul shall raise
one unending song of worship,
one unceasing hymn of praise,
celebrating God Eternal,
Lord of everlasting days.

Martin E. Leckebusch

Metre: 87 87 87
Suggested tune: *Rhuddlan*

Advent 3

Year B

Isaiah 61:1-4, 8-11
Psalm 126
or *Canticle:* Magnificat
1 Thessalonians 5:16-24
John 1:6-8, 19-28

He has sent me . . . to proclaim liberty to the captives, and release to the prisoners. (Isaiah 61:1c)

Prayer

At Advent we should try the key to our heart's door. It may have gathered rust. If so, this is the time to oil it, in order that the heart's door may open more easily when the Lord Jesus wants to enter at Christmas time!

Lord, oil the hinges of our hearts' doors that they may swing gently and easily to welcome your coming.

Prayer of a New Guinea Christian

Psalm 126

When you brought the captives home
it was a dream come true;
joy and laughter overflowed
in gratitude to you.

For in that call to freedom
a new life had begun,
and even non-believers
confessed what you had done!

All that you have done for us
has filled us with delight;
we have felt your tenderness
and seen your saving might.

But now our souls are barren,
our hearts are desert-dry;
renew us, Lord, revive us –
for streams of grace we cry.

When your servants go in tears
to sow their precious grain,
grant a joyful harvest-hymn
to lead them home again.

Martin E. Leckebusch

Metre: 76 76
Suggested tunes: *All Things Bright and Beautiful; Royal Oak*

Advent 3

Year C

Zephaniah 3:14-20
Canticle: Isaiah 12:2-6
Philippians 4:4-7
Luke 3:7-18

He will renew you in his love. (Zephaniah 3:17b)

Prayer

Eternal God,
we celebrate today
the fulfilment of your promises of old
through the coming of the Messiah,
foretold by the prophets and long yearned for –
a Saviour to deliver your people
and establish your kingdom,
bring freedom, life and new beginnings.
We celebrate how wonderfully you honoured those promises in Christ,
granting through him more than we can ever ask or imagine.
Help us now, as we worship you,
to celebrate your faithfulness
and to trust you completely for the future,
knowing that we can depend on you, come what may,
certain that what you have pledged will be accomplished
and that nothing can ever separate us from your love
in Jesus Christ our Lord.
Amen.

Nick Fawcett

Poem

You see me as no one else starts to,
the person concealed deep inside,
the weaknesses, faults and temptations,
the defects I'd much rather hide,
you see me laid bare of pretension,
the surface veneer stripped away,
the failings I cannot quite conquer
exposed to the cold light of day.
And yet you continue to love me,
your mercy and grace shining through;
despite all the times that I fail you,
you carry on making me new.
Such love is too awesome to credit,
like no other love that I know,
but though, Lord, I can't quite believe it,
you show me each day it is so.

Nick Fawcett

Advent 4

Year A

Isaiah 7:10-16
Psalm 80:1-8, 18-20
Romans 1:1-7
Matthew 1:18-25

An angel of the Lord appeared to Joseph in a dream. (Matthew 1:20)

Prayer

Blessed are you, Lord our God,
for in your love you wait on us.
You trust us with your plans
and allow us to share in the bringing in of your kingdom.
Help us at all times to trust in you
and to seek to do your will.
Blessed are you, Father, Son and Holy Spirit.

Lord, ever with us, help your Church
to proclaim your presence and your saving power.
May we seem to do your will
and help to bring in your kingdom.
As we give thanks for Joseph,
we give thanks for all men and women of vision
and all who have dedicated their lives in your service.
We ask your blessing upon all preachers
and ministers of the sacraments.
Guide all who serve you quietly in their daily lives.
We remember especially
all who struggle to serve you
while surrounded by difficult circumstances
and opposition.

God, come among us:
make your home with us.

Amen.

David Adam

Poem

Joseph was a good man.
It's hard to be a good man here below.
Joseph was true, true as a tree is true.
Joseph did what the angel told him to do.
When Mary needed his shelter, he was there,
strong as a tree, four square.
Joseph knew how to obey.
We'd call him Joe if he were living today . . .
'Hey, Joe, can you mend my hay rack?'
'Why, Joe, you've done a beautiful job on my chair!'
Yes, Joseph was a good man.
When God needed him, he was there.

Elizabeth Rooney

Advent 4

Year B

2 Samuel 7:1-11, 16
Canticle: Magnificat
or Psalm 89:1-4, 19-26
Romans 16:25-27
Luke 1:26-38

The angel came to her and said, "Greetings, favoured one! The Lord is with you."
(Luke 1:28)

Prayer

Almighty God,
we recall at this joyful season how,
through her willingness to hear your word
and commit herself to your service,
you were able to use Mary to fulfil your purpose,
entering our world,
inaugurating your kingdom
and bringing closer that day
when sorrow and suffering,
darkness and death
will be no more.
Help us, then, as we gather now to worship,
to hear your word
and to respond with similar obedience,
prepared to be used as you see fit.
Through our discipleship,
weak and feeble though it might be,
may your grace be revealed,
your love made known
and your world enriched.
Amen.

Nick Fawcett

Poem

There was
is
has been
and will be
an everywhere
fixed
and transfixed
within
that point in time
wherein
one single
simple
open soul
received
the potency
of the creative whole.

Elizabeth Rooney

Advent 4

Year C

Micah 5:2-5a
Canticle: Magnificat
or Psalm 80:1-8
Hebrews 10:5-10
Luke 1:39-45 (46-55)

When Elizabeth heard Mary's greeting, the child leapt in her womb. (Luke 1:41a)

Prayer

Almighty God,
you are greater than our minds can fathom,
higher than our highest thoughts,
sovereign over all,
worthy of praise and honour.
Forgive us that we sometimes lose
our sense of awe and wonder in your presence,
oblivious to your greatness and forgetful of your goodness.
Speak to us,
as you spoke to Mary,
and help us to catch a new sense of who you are,
of all you have done,
and of all you will yet do in our lives.
Help us to magnify your name,
singing your praises and telling of your greatness,
through Jesus Christ our Lord.
Amen.

Nick Fawcett

Poem

God was looking for a carpenter.
He wanted a skilled craftsman
to make him a cross.
The wood must be hard and wide,
straight cut with the joints perfectly squared
and planed as smooth as a yoke.
Finally, he needed a handful of nails
and then, God hung the perfect gift
upon the perfect tree –
Love, present with us through eternity.

Elizabeth Rooney

CHRISTMAS

Christmas Day

Years A, B and C

Any of the following sets of readings may be used on Christmas Day. Set III should be used at some service during the celebration.

I: Isaiah 9:2-7
Psalm 96
Titus 2:11-14
Luke 2:1-14 (15-20)

II: Isaiah 62:6-12
Psalm 97
Titus 3:4-7
Luke 2:(1-7) 8-20

III: Isaiah 52:7-10
Psalm 98
Hebrews 1:1-4 (5-12)
John 1:1-14

For a child has been born for us, a son given to us. (Isaiah 9:6a)

Prayer

Heavenly Father, we thank you for showing us your greatness in the helplessness of a newborn baby, your glory in the squalor of a cattle shed and your love in a poor peasant family who could find no room at the inn. May we welcome Christ into our lives and learn that real greatness lies in humble service, real glory is wrapped in holiness and real love shines like starlight, even in the darkest place. Amen.

Peter Dainty

Poem

When God was wrapping up the universe
he chose star-studded tissue for the sky,
a flowered-green for earth,
and blue foil shot with silver
for the sea.
He gave us everything –
even himself, the perfect gift of Love.
Surprising gift –
a baby wrapped in swaddling clothes,
lying on straw.

Elizabeth Rooney

First Sunday of Christmas

Year A

Isaiah 63:7-9
Psalm 148
Hebrews 2:10-18
Matthew 2:13-23

Then Joseph got up, took the child and his mother by night, and went to Egypt. (Matthew 2:14)

Prayer

Loving God,
remind us that in taking flesh and being born as a baby,
you identified yourself fully with humankind,
not imposing yourself upon us
but drawing alongside,
inviting a response.
Remind us that you made yourself vulnerable,
exposing yourself to persecution and rejection from the beginning,
willingly bearing the price of love.
Open our hearts today to respond –
freely, gladly and reverently –
ready to risk something for you
who risked so much for us.
Amen.

Nick Fawcett

Poem

There will be blood on the snow
beneath the Christmas moon.
gather the child and go.
Go soon!

Carry him safe to Egypt,
the child who came to save,
for the little boys of Bethlehem
will soon lie in their grave.

There will be weeping in the streets
beneath the winter sky.
Since Herod fears the holy child,
the Jewish child must die.

The child of peace is sleeping
on the Egyptian sands;
the sword he brought is reeking
in Herod's soldiers' hands.

Oh, child, who came to bring us
good tidings and great joys,
the families of Bethlehem
are weeping for their boys!

Elizabeth Rooney

First Sunday of Christmas

Year B

Isaiah 61:10 – 62:3
Psalm 148
Galatians 4:4-7
Luke 2:15-21

The shepherds returned, glorifying and praising God for all they had heard and seen.
(Luke 2:20)

Prayer

Lord Jesus Christ,
like the shepherds of old
we come with hearts ablaze
to celebrate your birth,
to kneel in wonder,
to offer our thanksgiving
and to respond personally to you.
May we, like them, thrill to the good news of your coming,
and go on our way rejoicing,
making known to those we meet
everything we have found to be true in you.
In your name we pray.
Amen.

Nick Fawcett

Poem

The shepherds watched their flocks by night,
and saw angels –
while townsmen, sleeping
in a noisier, narrower world,
blinkered against the light,
deaf to eternal voices,
waking only to complete the daily schedule,
saw and heard
nothing.

And the shepherds,
seeing angels,
did not then disperse the vision
with cool reason,
raising mental barricades
to blot out the light,
but received the message
with unquestioning joy,
open-mouthed,
yet speechless.

And these same poor shepherds,
unembarrassed by the stable
and the Saviour's poverty,
gladly adored him,
overawed by the very lowliness
which would have repelled
those richer in possessions,
but with ragged souls.

So the shepherds,
being ready to receive from God
with honest faith,
were as wise in their way
as the bringers of
gold, frankincense and myrrh.

Peter Dainty

First Sunday of Christmas

Year C

1 Samuel 2:18-20, 26
Psalm 148
Colossians 3:12-17
Luke 2:41-52

After three days they found him in the temple. (Luke 2:46a)

Prayer

Father God,
as you drew Jesus even as a child to your house,
to seek you there and learn more of your will,
so help us to sense your hand drawing us there
today,
to guide, challenge, nourish and nurture,
opening up new experiences of your love and
fresh insights in to your will.
Grant that we might approach you now,
not out of duty or habit
but hungry to meet with you once more,
to hear your voice
and to answer your call,
through Jesus Christ our Lord.
Amen.

Nick Fawcett

Poem

Beware, old men,
of the boy who asks questions
in the Temple.
Beware of his probing mind,
like the prodding finger of God
unplayfully poking holes
in your ancient dignity.
Hide those antique laws
before he sees the spirit
beneath the letter.
Protect those sacred truths with iron fear,
or he will fan them into life
with the breath of his living faith;
and the fire of their knowledge
will destroy both you
and your solemn system.
Beware of this boy who asks questions,
the inquisitive Son
of a disturbing Father.

Others there are
whom you need not fear –
they ask no questions,
but tread traditional ways
like sleep-walkers, blindly following
the easy path of custom,
each predictable today
a reprint of a ritual yesterday.

But this boy,
who so amazes with his insight,
is stirring the dust of ages
with the eternal broom of truth,
for he is God's boy,
already about his Father's business.

Peter Dainty

Second Sunday of Christmas

Years A, B and C

Jeremiah 31:7-14
Psalm 147:13-21
Ephesians 1:3-14
John 1: (1-9) 10-18

or

Ecclesiasticus 24:1-12
Canticle: Wisdom of
Solomon 10:15-21
Ephesians 1:3-14
John 1: (1-9) 10-18

They shall come and sing aloud on the height of Zion. (Jeremiah 31:12a)

Prayer

Creator God,
made known to us in the Word made flesh,
revealing your grace and truth through him
and bringing light into the darkness of our world,
come again to us now
and dwell among us through your Spirit.
Breathe life within us –
new life born not of the flesh but of you,
so that your Word might work within us,
speaking to our hearts,
illuminating our minds
and shining from our lives,
to your glory.
Amen.

Nick Fawcett

Poem

There had been stars
year after desert year,
a cold light
and a distant
for stars are never near.

Until the light
that lighted all the world
consented to be born.

The night he came
the stars swung low
and sang
as morning stars had sung
Creation's morn.

So sing we now.
Star-crossed,
we sing the bright
and morning star
shining among us,
banishing our night.

Elizabeth Rooney

EPIPHANY

Epiphany

Years A, B and C

Isaiah 60:1-6
Psalm 72:(1-9) 10-15
Ephesians 3:1-12
Matthew 2:1-12

They saw the child with Mary his mother; and they knelt down and paid him homage.
(Matthew 2:11a)

Prayer

Lord Jesus Christ,
hope of your people,
hope of your world,
touch now our lives as we gather before you.
Shine in our hearts,
illumine our minds
and light up our spirits,
so that we will grasp more clearly
the hope you give us in turn:
the assurance of your love
and the joy of life in all its fullness,
here now
and for all eternity.
Amen.

Nick Fawcett

Poem

What shall I bring you,
King, my king,
Creator and giver of everything?
What shall I bring?

Shall I bring you the work of my hands,
the gold
of all of the years of my growing old?
Shall I bring you gold?

Shall I bring you prayer,
the long intense
hours when silence grows immense,
when the spirit ascends like frankincense?
Shall I bring you prayer?

Shall I bring you myrrh,
the suffering with,
the learning to let each other live,
to care and to share and still forgive?
Shall I bring you myrrh?

What shall I bring you,
King, my king?
The love in my heart,
the songs I sing,
the will to obey you in everything.
These will I bring, O King, my king!

Elizabeth Rooney

The Baptism of Christ

First Sunday of Epiphany

Year A

Isaiah 42:1-9
Psalm 29
Acts 10:34-43
Matthew 3:13-17

God anointed Jesus of Nazareth with the Holy Spirit and with power. (Acts 10:38)

Prayer

Lord Jesus Christ
Redeemer,
deliverer,
we remember today your obedience to God's call –
your readiness to commit your life
to the way of service and sacrifice,
surrendering yourself in order to save others.
Challenge us through that example
to consider our own faith and calling:
the nature of our discipleship
and the priorities we set in our lives.
Help us, remembering all you have done for us
and celebrating the love you continue so
  constantly to show,
to commit ourselves again to the growth of your
  kingdom
on earth as it is in heaven.
Amen.

Nick Fawcett

Poem

Christ is our freedom: Christ who is Lord
shared in our life and died in our place.
Now he has paid the price for our sin,
clearing the way for pardon and grace:
holiness we could never achieve
comes as a gift to all who believe!

Christ is our freedom: there at the cross
he tore apart the shackles of sin:
now he has set the hostages free,
now resurrection life can begin.
Once we were slaves to sin and its powers –
now we are Christ's, and freedom is ours.

Christ is our freedom: Christ is alive!
Tough he was dead, in triumph he rose!
Into his Church his Spirit he pours,
bring his life as through us he flows –
we can enjoy the promised release:
lifted from guilty struggling to peace.

Christ is our freedom: baptism tells
what he has done, and what he will give:
buried with Christ, to him we belong;
he is our life – for him we now live,
trusting his promise, born of his word,
freed to be fruitful serving the Lord.

Martin E. Leckebusch

The Baptism of Christ

First Sunday of Epiphany

Year B

Genesis 1:1-5
Psalm 29
Acts 19:1-7
Mark 1:4-11

You are my Son, the beloved; with you I am well pleased. (Mark 1:11)

Prayer

Lord Jesus Christ,
we praise you today for your obedience to God's call,
your willingness to commit yourself
to the way of service, sacrifice and self-denial
so that we might become children of God.
Give us, as we worship you,
a clearer understanding of all that means –
the joy it offers and responsibility it entails –
so that we might commit ourselves more fully to you
and respond in turn to *your* call,
for your name's sake.
Amen.

Nick Fawcett

Psalm 29

The voice which shakes the earth
till mountains heave and quake,
the voice which causes ancient oaks
  to bend and break,
the voice which thunders loud
above the crashing waves
belongs to God, the Holy One,
  the Lord who saves.

When God's majestic voice
round hill and valley rings,
the desert blooms, the woodland skips,
  the forest sings:
his word proclaims the truth
like lightning, sharp and bright,
with penetrating clarity
  and tender might.

At his eternal throne
await the solemn sound,
for nowhere else will greater strength
  or peace be found.
Exalt the God of power,
and kneel in reverent fear –
give glory to the One whose voice
  we long to hear.

Martin E. Leckebusch

Metre: 66 84 D
Suggested tune: *Leoni*

The Baptism of Christ

First Sunday of Epiphany

Year C

Isaiah 43:1-7
Psalm 29
Acts 8:14-17
Luke 3:15-17, 21, 22

When you pass through the waters, I will be with you. (Isaiah 43:2a)

Prayer

O Christ, you humbled yourself
and received baptism at the hands of your friend
   and cousin, John,
showing us the way of humility;
help us to follow you,
and never to be encumbered with pride.

O Christ, by your baptism,
you took our humanity into the cleansing waters;
give us new birth,
and lead us into life as sons and daughters of God.

O Christ, by your baptism
the material world became charged with your
   holiness;
make us instruments of your transformation in
   this our world.

O Christ, by your baptism
you revealed the Trinity,
your Father calling you his beloved Son,
and the Spirit descending upon you like a dove;
renew our worship,
rededicate us in the spirit of our baptism,
and mould us into our true nature, in the image
   of God.
For your love's sake.

after the Chaldean Rite

Poem

However great the treasures life affords
in status or prosperity,
their transitory nature stands exposed:
they offer scant security.

We trust the Lord whose all-creating word
gave rise to wonders still unknown –
who holds unnumbered stars within his hand
yet loves to make our hearts his own.

Although we may be faced with many trials
and dangers often close at hand,
no peril we encounter has the power
to undermine what God has planned.

And so, in spite of all the grievous wounds
which mar a world whose pain we share,
we sense the details of our daily lives
are held within God's watchful care.

Martin E. Leckebusch

Second Sunday of Epiphany

Year A

Isaiah 49:1-7
Psalm 40:1-12
1 Corinthians 1:1-9
John 1:29-42

I myself have seen and have testified that this is the Son of God. (John 1:34)

Prayer

Gracious God,
help us, like John the Baptist before us
and so many others who have followed in his footsteps,
to see the light of Christ and bear witness to it,
pointing through word and deed to his love for all.
Open our lives, through your Spirit,
to his presence among us now,
and help us to live in such a way that his light may shine *in* us
and *through* us,
bringing glory to you.
Amen.

Nick Fawcett

Psalm 40

Out of life's quagmire I was rescued –
this is my song, my tale to tell:
hearing how you, Lord, answered my prayer,
others will honour you as well.
Blessed are those who choose to trust you,
leaving all other gods behind;
unnumbered miracles of mercy
such folk are privileged to find.

Should I rely on ritual offerings?
Would they be all that you require?
Have you not written life's instructions?
Your will, my God, is my desire!
You see my willingness to witness –
how could I hide your word away?
Love must be central to my lifestyle,
truth at the heart of all I say.

Yet, Lord, again I cry for mercy:
may truth and love enfold my life –
more sins are mine than I can number;
my days are seldom free of strife:
come quickly, Lord – my foes pursue me;
Show them how sin will bring them shame.
You are my rescuer and helper –
with all your saints I praise your name.

Martin E. Leckebusch

Metre: 98 98 D
Suggested tune: *Rendez à Dieu*

Second Sunday of Epiphany

Year B

1 Samuel 3:1-10 (11-20)
Psalm 139:1-5, 12-18
Revelation 5:1-10
John 1:43-51

Then the Lord called, 'Samuel! Samuel!' and he said, 'Here I am!'. (1 Samuel 3:4)

Prayer

Lord, you know me through and through,
every little thing I do,
when I work and when I rest,
when I'm happy, when depressed.
Lord, you know and understand;
hold me in your loving hand.

Lord, you know my every word
long before it's even heard.
You discern my thoughts and dreams,
all my secret plans and schemes.
Lord, you know and understand;
hold me in your loving hand.

Lord, wherever I may go,
speeding on or moving slow,
there I find you by my side,
present help and constant guide.
Lord, you know and understand;
hold me in your loving hand.

Lord, you formed me in the womb;
wove my being on life's loom.
Great and marvellous is your art,
far beyond all human thought.
Lord, you know and understand;
hold me in your loving hand.

Lord, examine my poor heart;
take away the evil part.
Lead me further, day by day,
in your everlasting way.
Lord, you know and understand;
hold me in your loving hand.

Peter Dainty

Psalm 139

My Lord, you have examined me,
you know me through and through;
you see my deeds, perceive my thoughts,
my speech, my motives too.
You wrap me round on every side;
on me you place your hand:
such knowledge is too wonderful
for me to understand!

The presence of your Spirit will
be with me to the last;
wherever I decide to go
your love will hold me fast.
If I should try to run from you
I know without a doubt
no darkness could conceal my path –
your light would shine me out.

You made me in my mother's womb,
so intricate your ways,
and even then, before my birth,
you numbered all my days.
Before I sleep and as I wake
I know that you are there:
how could I ever sound the depths
of your unfailing care?

And yet I find my soul perturbed
by bitterness and grief,
for many choose to treat your word
with scornful unbelief –
so search me, Lord, and cleanse my heart
from all that you abhor,
then teach me how to walk with you
today and evermore.

Martin E. Leckebusch

Metre: 86 86 D (DCM)
Suggested tune: *Kingsfold*

Second Sunday of Epiphany

Year C

Isaiah 62:1-5
Psalm 36:5-10
1 Corinthians 12:1-11
John 2:1-11

You have kept the good wine until now. (John 2:10b)

Prayer

Lord Jesus Christ,
come among us and, by your grace,
work your miracle of renewal once more in our
hearts.
Where the sparkle has gone out of life,
where joy is lacking,
where hope seems exhausted
or where resources seem to have run dry,
bring the wine of new life,
welling up within us
and bubbling over into spontaneous celebration,
resurgent faith
and confidence in your ability
to see us through to new beginnings.
In your name we ask it.
Amen.

Nick Fawcett

Poem

When the wine runs dry
at the festival of life,
when words fail, and music dies;
when our joys wear thin,
or old friendships end in strife,
and our laughter turns to sighs –
then come, Lord Jesus,
turn our water into wine,
as you turn the rain from heaven
to the sweetness of the vine;
turn the tears of our night
into songs of the day,
and revive us with your Spirit
as we walk the pilgrim way;
and baptise us with a fresh desire
to love you and obey –
Jesus, turn our water into wine.

When you took your towel and bowl
and you washed those weary feet,
you turned that water into wine.
And when we, at your command,
give a cup to cool the heat,
you turn that water into wine.
So come, Lord Jesus,
bring your heaven down to earth,
and fulfil the ancient prophecy
that at the world's new birth
every tear will be dried up
and there will be no more sea;
for we understand the reason
why such wonders have to be –
it's because you'll have completed
what began in Galilee:
you'll have turned all the water into wine.

Peter Dainty

Third Sunday of Epiphany

Year A

Isaiah 9:1-4
Psalm 27:1, 4-12
1 Corinthians 1:10-18
Matthew 4:12-23

The people who walked in darkness have seen a great light. (Isaiah 9:2a)

Prayer

Sovereign God,
without your light in our lives we walk in darkness,
denied the joy, peace, hope, strength and guidance
that you alone can give.
So we ask, through this time of worship,
that the light of Christ might break yet more fully
into our hearts
and shine more brightly through our lives,
to your glory.
Amen.

Nick Fawcett

Hymn

Where shadows once were found,
where death was loathed and feared,
where men and women lived in gloom
a light has now appeared.

To all our darkest paths
the light has found a way;
and nor can darkness master it –
the light has come to stay.

This light which we have seen
is Christ, and Christ alone:
by truth and grace the living Light
has made the Father known.

The brightness we had lost
in Christ is now restored:
believing human hearts reflect
the splendour of the Lord.

So in our daily lives
let grace and truth abound;
Lord, by your Spirit shine through us
where shadows once were found.

Martin E. Leckebusch

Metre: 6 6 8 6 (SM)
Suggested tune: *Sandys*

Third Sunday of Epiphany

Year B

Genesis 14:17-20
Psalm 128
Revelation 19:6-10
John 2:1-11

Blessed are those who are invited to the marriage supper of the Lamb. (Revelation 19:9)

Prayer

Lord Jesus Christ,
remind us afresh today of your transforming power,
your ability to take something ordinary
and turn it into something special.
Take, then, our worship,
and, by your Spirit,
make it into something beautiful to you,
bringing you glory
and stirring again our hearts within us.
Take our lives,
and by your Spirit once more create us anew,
so that our lives will speak not of our weakness
but of your saving love and gracious power,
to the glory of your name.
Amen.

Nick Fawcett

Psalm 128

Whoever fears the Lord
and lives as he intends
will find the whole of life
is filled with gifts he sends.

When work is more than toil
and reaps a just reward,
when strength and health are ours,
all these are from the Lord!

We celebrate the joys
of home and family,
where love's enduring bonds
provide security.

God nurtures every child
for life's demanding race;
each day he offers us
new fruitfulness, new grace.

His kindness is revealed
where bitter conflicts cease;
far more, within our hears,
his mercy brings us peace.

May God prolong our days
to see our children's heirs,
and may his gracious gifts
be ours and also theirs.

Martin E. Leckebusch

Metre: 66 66
Suggested tune: *Ibstone*

Third Sunday of Epiphany

Year C

Nehemiah 8:1-3, 5, 6, 8-10
Psalm 19
1 Corinthians 12:12-31a
Luke 4:14-21

He went to the synagogue on the sabbath day. (Luke 4:16)

Prayer

Lord Jesus Christ,
as you expounded the Scriptures during your
earthly ministry,
unfolding their true meaning,
so, we ask, unfold them to us now,
through your Spirit.
Help us to grasp more clearly
the nature of your kingdom,
the extent of your love,
and the responsibilities that Christian
commitment entails,
both to you and others.
Save us from closing our ears
to that which challenges and disturbs,
stretching our horizons
and questioning comfortable assumptions.
Open our minds and hearts
to all you would say to us,
for your name's sake.
Amen.

Nick Fawcett

Psalm 19

The heavens proclaim God's glory,
the skies sing out in praise,
extolling their creator
through endless nights and days.
More eloquent than language,
more radiant than the sun,
this message of God's splendour
is meant for everyone.

The law of God is perfect,
its precepts always right,
revealing timeless wisdom,
providing life and light –
no gold could be so precious,
no honey taste as sweet;
and those who yield obedience
will find their joy complete.

Forgive my secret failures,
the faults I do not know;
from wilful sins protect me,
and ways I should not go.
May all my meditations,
my every thought and word,
be fashioned for your pleasure,
my Saviour and my Lord.

Martin E. Leckebusch

Metre: 76 76 D
Suggested tune: *St Theodulph*

Fourth Sunday of Epiphany

Year A

1 Kings 17:8-16
Psalm 36:5-10
1 Corinthians 1:18-31
John 2:1-11

The jar of meal was not emptied, neither did the jug of oil fail. (1 Kings 17:16a)

Prayer

Lord Jesus Christ,
take the water of our worship and our lives,
and turn it into wine.
Through your gracious touch,
transform what we are
and all we offer
into something special,
honouring to you and pleasing in your sight.
Work your miracle within us
as a sign of the new life you offer to all.
In your name we pray.
Amen.

Nick Fawcett

Poem

In the passionate care of a mother
and the heartfelt concern of a friend,
in the tender embrace of a lover,
in commitment that nothing can end,
I glimpse, gracious God, just a fraction
of the place I enjoy in your heart,
of your love shown so clearly in action
breaking down all that keeps us apart:
your sacrifice – suffering and dying –
to draw us once more to your side,
your mercy that never stops trying,
your purpose that won't be denied.
Such wonderful love leaves me reeling,
amazed it can ever be true.
Lord, grant me the same depth of feeling
in all of my dealings with you.

Nick Fawcett

Fourth Sunday of Epiphany

Year B

Deuteronomy 18:15-20
Psalm 111
Revelation 12:1-5a
Mark 1:21-28

And the unclean spirit, throwing him into convulsions and crying with a loud voice, came out of him. (Mark 1:26)

Prayer

Lord Jesus Christ,
as crowds in Galilee marvelled at your words and
deeds,
recognising in you an authority
unlike anything they had seen before,
speaking powerfully of God's gracious purpose
and involvement in their lives,
so, we pray, minister to us now,
speaking again your redeeming word
and revealing once more your renewing power.
Open our eyes
to your saving grace and healing love,
to all you are doing in our lives and our world,
so that the gospel might come alive for us each day,
ringing true in our daily experience,
causing us to marvel and rejoice in turn,
giving thanks for the evidence you give
of God's voice speaking afresh
and his hand at work among us.
Amen.

Nick Fawcett

Psalm 111

I will stand with God's people and pour out my
praise;
I delight in the wonders the Lord has made known,
for righteousness echoes through all that he says,
and his deeds have a splendour which mirrors his own.

They will not be forgotten, the things he has done,
for as he rules the nations his power is displayed.
In all that he gives us his kindness is seen;
he will always be true to each promise he made.

As the fear of the Lord is where wisdom begins,
let his precepts instruct us, directing our ways.
So awesome he is, and so holy and just:
let eternity ring with the sound of his praise!

Martin E. Leckebusch

Metre: 12 12 11 12
Suggested tune: *Stowey*

Fourth Sunday of Epiphany

Year C

Ezekiel 43:27 – 44:4
Psalm 48
1 Corinthians 13:1-13
Luke 2:22-40

The glory of the Lord filled the temple of the Lord; and I fell upon my face.
(Ezekiel 44:4b)

Prayer

Almighty God, whose Son our Saviour Jesus Christ is the light of the world: grant that we and all your people may shine with the radiance of his glory, that he may be known, worshipped, and obeyed to the ends of the earth; through Jesus Christ our Lord, who with you and the Holy Spirit lives and reigns, on God, now and for Ever.

Episcopal Church, USA

Poem

O splendour of God's glory bright,
who bringest forth the light from Light;
O Light, of light the fountain-spring;
O Day, our days illumining;
come, very Sun of truth and love,
come in thy radiance from above,
and shed the Holy Spirit's ray
on all we think or do today.

St Ambrose

The Presentation of Christ in the Temple

Years A, B and C

Malachi 3:1-5
Psalm 24:(1-6), 7-10
Hebrews 2:14-18
Luke 2:22-40

For my eyes have seen your salvation. (Luke 2:30)

Prayer

Blessed are you Lord our God.
To you be all praise and glory for ever and ever,
for you are our light and our salvation.
You created light out of darkness
and have brought your light to our lives
through the birth of your Son, our Lord Jesus Christ.
Blessed are you, Father, Son and Holy Spirit,
one God for ever and ever.

As our Lord was brought into the Temple,
we ask your blessing upon the Church
throughout the world.
May we share in the mission of Christ
and show that his light is for all peoples and nations.
We remember all who are being baptised or
confirmed
and all who are seeking to dedicate their lives
in your service.
We pray for all your faithful people,
that they may be lights in the world.

Lord of light and life,
hear our prayer.

Amen.

David Adam

Poem

Now, Lord, please let your servant go in peace;
your ancient promise is at last fulfilled.
My eyes have seen salvation in this child,
whom you have sent in love for all mankind.
His light reveals your truth in every land;
the brightest gem in Israel's crown is he.
His love will move the heart of all the world,
until his Spirit fills earth, sky and sea.

Peter Dainty

ORDINARY TIME

Proper 1

Year A

Isaiah 58:1-9a (9b-12)
Psalm 112:1-9 (10)
1 Corinthians 2:1-12 (13-16)
Matthew 5:13-20

Share your bread with the hungry, and bring the homeless poor into your house.
(Isaiah 58:7a)

Prayer

Lord Jesus Christ,
as you taught the crowds on the mountaintop,
so now teach us as we gather in your name.
Prompt us through your Spirit,
that we might hear and understand your word.
Help us to listen and learn,
reflecting on what you say to us
and applying it to our lives,
so that our words and deeds
might bear witness to you,
your light shining through us,
to the glory of God the Father.
Amen.

Nick Fawcett

Hymn

O Lord, I want to praise you,
your holy name confess,
your mighty deeds acknowledge,
your awesome love express.
I want to give you honour,
to lift your name on high,
yet somehow words are lacking
however hard I try.

I want so much to thank you
through all I say and do,
to so live out the gospel
that all may know it's true.
I yearn to give you glory,
to help your kingdom grow,
yet though I strive to serve you
it rarely seems to show.

I bring you, Lord, my service,
deficient though it be;
aware my faults are many,
I come still, joyfully.
For though I'm weak and foolish
and know you but in part,
you look beneath the surface
and see what's in the heart.

Nick Fawcett

Metre: 7 6 7 6 D
Suggested tune: *Ellacombe*

Proper 1

Year B

Isaiah 40:21-31
Psalm 147:1-12, 20c
1 Corinthians 9:16-23
Mark 1:29-39

*Those who wait for the Lord shall renew their strength,
they shall mount up with wings like eagles.* (Isaiah 40:31a)

Prayer

Gracious God,
may the good news of Jesus Christ
thrill us again as we worship you;
may the message of his saving power
kindle fresh faith within us;
may the touch of his hand
bring us new beginnings;
may the experience of his love send us on our way,
restored,
made whole.
Open our lives to the wonder of the gospel,
so that, experiencing the joy and fulfilment it brings,
we may share it with others,
helping them too to know the truth
and experience your love for themselves,
to the glory of your name.
Amen.

Nick Fawcett

Psalm 147

With hallelujahs honour God,
his wisdom and his might:
you saints, extol the Righteous One
who formed and named each star,
who knows the pain of every wound,
who heals the deepest scar,
who gathers exiles home again –
his praise is our delight.

Bring skilful tunes and thankful words:
for clouds that soar above,
for food to nourish bird and beast,
for every gassy hill;
yet neither nature's finest joys
nor human strength or skill
can bring the Lord such happiness
as hearts that trust his love.

He sends the snow – then at his word
the springtime is restored
as icy blast and wintry chill
succumb to warmth and life;
but more than this, his word to us
brings peace in place of strife;
you saints, let hallelujahs sound
in honour of the Lord.

Martin E. Leckebusch

Metre: 86 86 D (DCM)
Suggested tune: *Kingsfold*

Proper 1
Year C

Isaiah 6:1-8 (9-13)
Psalm 138
1 Corinthians 15:1-11
Luke 5:1-11

They caught so many fish that their nets were beginning to break. (Luke 5:6)

Prayer

Lord Jesus Christ,
remind us again today that,
unworthy though we are,
you have called us to faith and discipleship,
to be your witnesses here on earth.
Equip us, then, to honour you,
for we cannot do so alone,
there being so little right in us
and so much wrong.
Speak once more your word of call,
of mercy
and of life,
and send us out to serve you,
in your strength
and for your kingdom's sake.
Amen.

Nick Fawcett

Poem

Lord of life, direct my ways,
help me love you all my days.
Though my faith is flowed and frail,
though I all too often fail,
take my heart, my hands, my feet –
reach out now to all I meet.
Teach me how to serve and when.
Guide my footsteps, Lord. Amen.

Nick Fawcett

Proper 2

Year A

Deuteronomy 30:15-20
or Ecclesiasticus 15:15-20
Psalm 119:1-8
1 Corinthians 3:1-9
Matthew 5:21-37

Choose life so that you and your descendants may live. (Deuteronomy 30:19b)

Prayer

Gracious God,
we mean to be faithful to you,
to live as you have called us to,
but somehow we repeatedly end up
turning the positive message of the gospel
into a list of negatives,
a matter of rules and regulations
rather than grateful response,
a law that imprisons
rather than a love that liberates.
Forgive us,
and teach us again your way –
the way of mercy and understanding
that leads to life.
In Christ's name we pray.
Amen.

Nick Fawcett

Hymn

Here is the route laid out for us to follow:
your word reveals the path we ought to tread.
You teach us how to walk and run in freedom
when by the truth we let ourselves be led –
so now we pledge to turn our backs on falsehood,
and to be guided by your law instead.

Here is the spring which offers real refreshment
to weary hearts, worn down by endless strain:
within your word we find such inspiration,
and ample strength to bear our deepest pain.
Lord, in our lives renew your gracious promise
and speak the word which makes us strong again.

Here is the lamp by whose illumination
your holy ways lie open to our sight;
here are the keys of knowledge and discernment:
through your commands you show us what is
right;
so, Lord, behind the searching beam of Scripture
we look for you, the Source of perfect light.

Martin E. Leckebusch

Metre: 11 10 11 10 11 10
Suggested tune: *Finlandia*

Proper 2

Year B

2 Kings 5:1-14
Psalm 30
1 Corinthians 9:24-27
Mark 1:40-45

Moved with pity, Jesus stretched out his hand and touched him. (Mark 1:41a)

Prayer

Lord Jesus, touch our eyes,
as you did those of the blind;
then we shall see
in things that are visible
those things which are invisible.
Lord Jesus, open our ears,
heal our wounds and purify our lives,
as you did those who came to you;
then we shall hear and perceive what is true
amidst the sounds of the world,
and find wholeness in ourselves.

after Origen (185-254)

Poem

Jesus was not afraid
to touch people;
not with the formal handshake of greeting,
or the limp clasp of indifference;
not with the vicious jab of hate,
the lascivious stroke of lust,
or greed's sweaty clutch;
but with the gentle touch
of fingers on blind eyes,
deaf ears and speechless tongues;
the touch that healed.
His reassuring grasp
cleansed scaly leprous hands.
His grip was strong enough
to put the lame on their feet
and free the paralysed.

Let those of us
whose fingers touch, not other fingers,
but computer buttons;
who hide behind a barrier
of printed words,
instructions and reports,
or the armchair newspaper;
who never actually meet
the needs of our neighbour,
except through collection boxes
held in the gloved hands of charity;
who are divided from others
by stone walls
or wooden pews
or windscreens
and well-trimmed hedges,
remember that Jesus Christ,
the Word made flesh,
the very hand of God,
was not afraid to touch
people.

Nor was Jesus afraid
to be touched
by people;
not just the accidental jostle
of the anonymous crowd
(though even that could help);
nor the playful prods of children
(though he would not turn them away),
but even the soldiers' rough brutality,
the stinging slaps and cold spittle
of Pilate's grinning henchmen;
the bitter kiss of a traitor,
and the burning talons
of the crucifiers.

So Christ's Body still
reaches out to those
who ache for love.
Nor should it shrink back
from the world's unfeeling blows,
but, turning cheek,
use even that as
saving contact.

Peter Dainty

Proper 2
Year C

Jeremiah 17:5-10
Psalm 1
1 Corinthians 15:12-20
Luke 6:17-26

Blessed are those who trust in the Lord, whose trust is the Lord.
They shall be like a tree planted by water, sending out its roots by the stream.
(Jeremiah 17:7, 8)

Prayer

Lord Jesus Christ,
we want to worship you
not through fine-sounding words or empty ritual
but through truly living as your people,
walking in your way and honouring your will.
Help us to understand what it means
to be part of your kingdom here on earth;
to recognise that it turns so many of our aspirations
and assumptions upside down.
Equip us not only to grasp that truth,
but also to apply it to daily life,
so that we might find in you
true riches and fulfilment,
lasting joy and love,
life able to satisfy not just now but for all eternity.
Amen.

Nick Fawcett

Psalm 1

A depth of satisfaction:
the promise is made known
to all who turn from evil
and make the Lord their own;
who heed no wicked counsel,
no cynic's mocking voice;
whose way of living signals
obedience as their choice.

The man or woman choosing
to follow what is right
will find God's word becoming
a source of pure delight:
here meditation causes
the finest fruit to grow
as when a tree is planted
where streams of water flow.

To trust in God will give us
a grounding firm and sure;
to disregard his wisdom
would make us insecure;
Lord, let us not be worthless
like chaff that blows away –
but guide us and protect us;
watch over us each day.

Martin E. Leckebusch

Metre: 76 76 D
Suggested tunes: *Crüger; Ellacombe*

Proper 3

Year A

Leviticus 19:1, 2, 9-18
Psalm 119:33-40
1 Corinthians 3:10, 11, 16-23
Matthew 5:38-48

But I say to you, love your enemies and pray for those who persecute you.
(Matthew 5:44)

Prayer

Living God,
we want to love *you*,
we want to love *others*,
but we're not very good at doing either.
Today, as we worship you,
teach us more of what love really means.
Speak to us through Christ,
and, through your Holy Spirit, equip us to follow his way,
turning the other cheek,
going the extra mile,
praying for our enemies,
giving without counting the cost.
Help us to love as fully as you love us,
to your glory.
Amen.

Nick Fawcett

Poem

My Father, full of endless love,
compassionate and kind,
to your unchanging faithfulness
no limits can I find.

In Christ you showed your care for all,
both crowds and those alone –
whatever human needs he found,
he made your kindness known.

Now may your Spirit touch my heart
with love's consuming fire:
creative, kind and thoughtful deeds
within my life inspire.

With stranger, friend and foe alike
your kindness I would share;
this fruit your Spirit nurtures, Lord,
is one I long to bear.

Martin E. Leckebusch

Metre: 8 6 8 6 (CM)
Suggested tune: *St Agnes (Dykes)*

Proper 3

Year B

Isaiah 43:18-25
Psalm 41
2 Corinthians 1:18-22
Mark 2:1-12

When Jesus saw their faith, he said to the paralytic, 'Son, your sins are forgiven'. (Mark 2:5)

Prayer

Sovereign God,
we come to you conscious of all that is wrong in our lives,
aware that we have no claim on your goodness
nor any merit that might lead us to expect it.
Yet we come knowing that you are a God of love,
slow to anger and swift to show mercy;
a God who yearns to put the past behind us
and to help us start again,
if only we are truly sorry and sincerely wish it.
So, then, we dare to approach,
trusting in your gracious love, so wonderfully revealed in Christ,
and, in penitence, seeking forgiveness and new beginnings.
Through your Son, put your hand upon us,
lift us up,
restore us
and send us on our way to live and work for you,
in his name.
Amen.

Nick Fawcett

Psalm 41

Teach me, Lord, your compassion
for those worn down by strain:
by raging conflicts all around,
by searing inner pain;
for I will need your comfort
when trouble reaches me –
when pressure and ill-health expose
how fragile life can be.

May I avoid the outlook
which always thinks of blame,
of seeing others' sufferings
as proof of guilty shame;
nor let me be the reason
for friendships torn in two –
no slander spread, no trust abused,
in what I say and do.

For times when I have failed you
I ask your mercy, Lord;
for grace to lead a fruitful life,
and peace in you restored;
so let me walk before you
in full integrity,
to worship you throughout my days
and all eternity.

Martin E. Leckebusch

Metre: 76 86 D
Suggested tune: *Alford*

Proper 3

Year C

Genesis 45:3-11, 15
Psalm 37:1-11, 40, 41
1 Corinthians 15:35-8, 42-50
Luke 6:27-38

I am your Brother Joseph, whom you sold into Egypt. (Genesis 45:4b)

Prayer

God remembers our frailty;
let us pray to him now.

When conflicts threaten to disrupt our fellowship
in the church community,
deal with our frustrations and anger,
and give us the grace to forgive.

Silence

May we love one another:
as you have loved us.

When the luggage we carry from the past
interferes with our capacity to cope with the present,
heal the damage from our memories
and transform our experiences for good.

Silence

May we love one another:
as you have loved us.

When the difference in cultures
block our understanding of one another
and obstruct the peace process,
broaden our vision to discern the common ground.

Silence

May we love one another:
as you have loved us.

When the layers of resentment
have turned into rock,
dissolve them with the rain of your loving mercy.

Silence

May we love one another:
as you have loved us.

As those we have known and loved
pass through the gate of death,
have mercy on them,
and receive them into the joy
of your eternal kingdom.

Silence

May we love one another:
as you have loved us.

As we acknowledge the beauty
of loving even our enemies,
we thank you for the extraordinary love
your show us in Jesus.

Merciful Father,
accept these prayers
for the sake of your Son,
our Saviour Jesus Christ. Amen.

Susan Sayers

Poem

I'm not an angel, nowhere near,
I often go astray,
but though my faults are all too clear,
I try, Lord, to obey.
Avoid what's evil, strive for good,
that's been my daily aim –
to live the sort of life I should
in keeping with your name.
But now I see that this alone
can never fully do;
instead it's how much love I've shown
that matters most to you –
if, when I saw a friend in need,
a person in despair,
I paid their plight sufficient heed,
enough to show I care.
My times of worship, hymns and prayers
each have their part to play,
but only if my life declares
the truth of what I say;
if what I am and what I do
stays faithful to your fall,
in showing love not just to you
but equally to all.

Nick Fawcett

Second Sunday before Lent

Year A

Genesis 1:1 – 2:3
Psalm 136 or Psalm 136:1-9, 23-26
Romans 8:18-25
Matthew 6:25-34

In the beginning . . . God created the heavens and the earth. (Genesis 1:1)

Prayer

Blessed are you, Lord God,
Giver of life and Creator of love.
We give you thanks and praise
for the light of each day
and for the light of the Gospel
as revealed in our Saviour Jesus Christ.
We rejoice in the life that you give us
and we delight in your presence.
Blessed are you, Father, Son and Holy Spirit.

As we give thanks for the light of Jesus Christ
we ask that this light may shine in our lives
and in the whole Church.
We ask your blessing
on all who proclaim the Gospel
and who teach the word.
We pray for all who are seeking
to revive and promote faith in you and your love.
May the Church grow in love, in witness and in number.

Lord God of light,
scatter the darkness from our world.
Amen.

David Adam

Poem

Across the boundless breadth of space,
assigning every star its place,
Lord God, your sovereign hand we trace –
and offer you our worship.

Your vast design is evident
on every isle and continent
where nature, so luxuriant,
inspires our hearts to worship.

You fashion rain and frost and snow,
make sun to blaze and wind to blow,
till garden, field and forest grow –
with thankful hearts we worship.

So many species, formed to fill
both sea and air, both plain and hill!
For all your rich creative skill
we lift our hearts in worship.

Can our lives then elude your sight?
Your love sustains us day and night!
To you, our Saviour, Lord, Delight,
we gladly bring our worship.

Martin E. Leckebusch

Second Sunday before Lent

Year B

Proverbs 8:1, 22-31
Psalm 104:24-35
Colossians 1:15-20
John 1:1-14

All things came into being through him, and without him not one thing came into being. (John 1:3)

Prayer

Sovereign God –
mighty and mysterious,
immortal,
invisible –
as we come together in your presence
we do not simply want to go through the motions
of worship,
to do what's expected of us;
we want to see Jesus,
recognising him at work in the world
and involved in our lives,
present and active through his Spirit.
Broaden our vision and enlarge our
understanding,
that we might glimpse more of his grace and truth,
love and light,
power and glory,
and so catch clearer sight also of you,
our eyes opened to your awesome majesty
through him.
Amen.

Nick Fawcett

Poem

Lord of all, we praise your name for your
creative love,
from which has flowed the whole miraculous,
glorious multiplicity of things
from atoms to galaxies, from dewdrops to oceans,
from nodding flowers to twinkling stars,
from sparking fireflies to blazing suns.
We praise you for this outpouring of your very self
in the beauty, joy, light and life of the world,
in the music of the spheres,
in the drama of universal history.

Creator of all things visible:
we praise your holy name.

And we praise you too for all invisible things –
for what cannot be touched, weighed or
measured, bought or sold,
but without which life would be poor and mean –
for friendship and love, kindness and courage,
generosity and encouragement;
for lofty ideals of justice and mercy;
for reason and curiosity;
for a sense of beauty and a sense of humour.

Creator all things invisible:
we praise your holy name.

Creator of all things seen and unseen,
we thank you for revealing yourself
in Jesus Christ, your visible image –
a man of flesh and blood,
living in the world of the five senses,
yet living and dying and rising again
by the power of the unseen Spirit,
that we might receive life in all its fullness.
Amen.

Peter Dainty

Second Sunday before Lent

Year C

Genesis 2:4b-9, 15-25
Psalm 65
Revelation 4
Luke 8:22-25

And he woke up and rebuked the wind and the raging waves. (Luke 8:24b)

Prayer

Living God,
we come in faith to worship you,
yet we come also conscious that our faith is so very weak,
all too easily undermined in the storms of life,
sinking without trace when trouble and danger threatens.
Forgive us,
and speak again of your loving purpose and sovereign power.
Teach us that even in times of turmoil you are there,
nothing finally able to overcome your will,
and in that confidence may we put our trust now and always.
Amen.

Nick Fawcett

Hymn

Lord, you created a world rich in splendour,
touched with a beauty no words can express,
able to move me to outbursts of wonder,
so much to savour and so much to bless.

Mountains and moorlands rise up to the heavens,
rivers and streams tumble down to the sea,
gifts that amaze in profusion surround me,
each a reflection of your majesty.

Promise of springtime and harvest of autumn,
old winter mornings and warm summer days,
season by seasons brings cause for rejoicing,
reason to thank you and reason to praise.

Deep in the forest, remote in the desert,
down in the ocean or high in the air;
life in abundance is everywhere round me,
proof of your power and sign of your care.

Lord, you have given a world rich in splendour,
touched with a beauty that fills me with awe;
hear now my praises, I bring you my worship,
with all creation I kneel and adore.

Nick Fawcett

Metre: 11 10 11 10
Suggested tune: *Epiphany*

Sunday next before Lent

Year A

Exodus 24:12-18
Psalm 2 or Psalm 99
2 Peter 1:16-21
Matthew 17:1-9

Moses went up into the mountain of God. (Exodus 24:13b)

Prayer

Lord Jesus Christ,
as we come to worship,
give us a sense of awe and wonder,
an awareness of the privilege we have in
knowing you,
receiving your Spirit
and being called your people.
Grant us a glimpse of your glory
that brings home to us
your greatness and goodness,
care and compassion,
purpose and pardon –
a foretaste that fills us with joy
and causes us to kneel in adoration,
overcome with amazement, thankfulness and love.
Teach us never to become casual in our devotion,
blasé, complacent or indifferent,
but to come rather with reverence and humility,
eager to offer you, through word and deed,
the adulation you deserve.
In your name we pray.
Amen.

Nick Fawcett

Hymn

Christ our Lord, we worship you,
for you left eternal glory,
taking mortal flesh and blood,
born to share our human story;
hallelujah!

Some who climbed a mountain high
glimpsed the truth – and fell, dumbfounded:
was your honour not disclosed
when the Father's voice resounded?
Hallelujah!

Yet a greater glory shone
when you faced humiliation,
when you suffered in our place,
crucified for our salvation;
hallelujah!

And your resurrection proved
sin's oppressive grasp was ended,
for you rose as living Lord
and in triumph you ascended;
hallelujah!

What a hope we now possess,
far surpassing earthly measure
for your Spirit thrills our hearts
with a taste of heaven's treasure!
Hallelujah!

When in splendour you return
every knee shall bow before you!
Come, our King, and take your throne –
hallelujah! We adore you!
Hallelujah!

Martin E. Leckebusch

Metre: 7 8 7 8 4
Suggested tune: *St Albinus*

Sunday next before Lent

Year B

2 Kings 2:1-12
Psalm 50:1-6
2 Corinthians 4:3-6
Mark 9:2-9

Elijah ascended in a whirlwind into heaven. (2 Kings 2:11b)

Prayer

Lord Jesus Christ,
however much we think we know you,
however clearly we believe we have understood
your greatness,
open our eyes today to a deeper awareness,
fuller picture
and yet more wonderful vision of who and what
you are.
Teach us that our minds can only begin to grasp
your glory,
at best glimpsing part of the truth,
for there is always more to be revealed,
more to learn,
more to catch our imagination and thrill our souls.
Grant then, as we worship you,
that your radiance might burst afresh into our lives,
so that we might return to the daily routine
determined to know, love and serve you better,
to the glory of your name.
Amen.

Nick Fawcett

Poem

Quietly, quietly he comes.
The sound of shaken silver starts
to ring within our hearts.
A sweetness steals
out of the quietness
and heals.
We are alive
with an intensity of joy
we had not dreamed.
And everything that seemed
to matter
matters now both more and less
here in the presence
of his holiness.

Elizabeth Rooney

Sunday next before Lent

Year C

Exodus 34:29-35
Psalm 99
2 Corinthians 3:12 – 4:2
Luke 9:28-36 (37-43a)

And while he was praying, the appearance of his face changed, and his clothes became dazzling white. (Luke 9:29)

Prayer

Sovereign God,
as Peter, James and John caught a glimpse of your radiance on the mountaintop,
revealed in Christ,
so may we today see your glory more clearly –
your light shining in our hearts,
firing our imagination,
filling us with joy
and fanning the flames of faith.
Help us, confronted by the mystery and wonder of your presence,
to recognise that,
however much we have understood,
you have far more to reveal,
our grasp of your greatness and experience of your love still partial,
needing always to be open to new horizons.
Speak, then,
and open our eyes,
in the name of Christ.
Amen.

Nick Fawcett

Poem

The mountain flames with light
as Christ, heaven's window,
opens this dark world
to divine glory.
He glows with a strange radiance
normally hidden
from earthbound eyes,
but now revealed
to dull disciples
facing the unknown.

And meanwhile,
down in the valley,
not lit by other worlds,
untransfigured suffering
distorts humanity.
Wretched bearer of pain
cry out for healing.
Well-meaning helpers
offer ineffectual suggestions,
while bystanders move in
with trivial objections.
Unillumined disciples
fail
and turn away,
embarrassed and ashamed.
Is their faith
not even the size
of a mustard seed?

Our earthly light is not enough,
unless transfigured
by the light from heaven.
Thank God that Christ's true glory
was not left to be enshrined
on some irrelevant mountain top;
but he came down
into the valley
to embrace the human beast
with arms stretched out
in sacrificial love,
that we might share
this royal beauty,
and dark earth at last
be radiant with heaven.

Peter Dainty

LENT

First Sunday of Lent

Year A

Genesis 2:15-17; 3:1-7
Psalm 32
Romans 5:12-19
Matthew 4:1-11

So when the woman saw that the tree was good for food . . .
she took of its fruit and ate. (Genesis 3:6)

Prayer

Search us, O God, and know our thoughts.
Examine us and reveal our faults.
Cleanse us and make us new.
Touch us and make us whole.
Equip us and give us strength.
Meet us and speak your word.
Hear us and accept our worship,
in Jesus' name.
Amen.

Nick Fawcett

Poem

If the innocent Woman of Eden
could suddenly hear
the voice of the Serpent
coming from nowhere,
and tempting her
to defy the will of God,
how much more can we
less innocent ones
still hear
the subtle Serpent's
seductive whisper
calling us
from the dark undergrowth
of our unsuspecting minds?

'Surely your freedom must not be denied.
If God knows best, then you,
made in his image,
must be allowed to know
as much as he.
The truth is beautiful,
and knowledge is so sweet.
Just taste and see.
It is a lie to say
that ignorance is bliss.
God seeks to keep control
and must impose this prohibition
on the human soul;
or it is God who'll die,
not you.
Throw off his chains.
Show that the human spirit reigns.
Let all the earth rejoice
in mankind's better world!'

Thus speaks the Serpent's voice;
and we, renouncing God,
now labour to produce
a better life,
at least for some.
But lust and pride have led
to hate and fear,
and poverty, injustice,
greed and war remain.
Yet, hiding from our God
in guilt and shame,
can we not hear,
even at this late hour,
not now the Serpent's poisonous hiss,
but God's more passionate, searching call:
'People of earth,
where are you?'

Peter Dainty

First Sunday of Lent

Year B

Genesis 9:8-17
Psalm 25:1-9
1 Peter 3:18-22
Mark 1:9-15

I have set my bow in the clouds, and it shall be a sign of the covenant between me and the earth. (Genesis 9:13)

Prayer

Blessed are you, Lord God, Creator of the universe.
You have given us this world to enjoy
and so that we may work in harmony with you.
You have given us talents and abilities
that we may enrich each other.
Blessed are you, Lord God.

Show us your ways, O Lord,
and teach us your paths.
Amen.

David Adam

Poem

God led Noah safely through the flood,
from the plains of Mesopotamia
to the mountains of Ararat.
It was a voyage between two worlds –
from the primitive world
of myth and legend,
the world of gods and giants,
into the world we know
and now inhabit,
the world of rules and rulers.

Eden's age of innocence
(so the story goes)
had given way,
to an unruly age
of violence
and corruption.
But the great Flood
put an end to all that.
And after the Flood,
there was law
based on strict justice –
a life for a life.
It was the beginning
of social order and control,
and we, the descendants of Noah,
have inherited his world,
although we've come a long way
since then.

Even the animals
were now ruled by fear.
Their flesh could be eaten,
and their bodies offered
in sacrifice.
Yet the eating of blood
was forbidden,
because the blood was the life,
and all life was sacred.
But we've come a long way
since then.

By the rainbow covenant,
God promised
the stability of nature –
enough to make possible
the unsteady growth
of human civilisation.
'Never again,' said God,
'will I destroy
all living creatures;
and seedtime and harvest,
cold and heat,
summer and winter,
day and night
will remain
as long as the earth endures.'
Oh glorious promise!

And we can surely trust God
not to break that promise.
The worry now is –
because we've come a long way
since the days of Noah –
can we trust *ourselves*
not to break God's promise
for him?

Peter Dainty

First Sunday of Lent

Year C

Deuteronomy 26:1-11
Psalm 91:1, 2, 9-16
Romans 10:8b-13
Luke 4:1-13

If you, then, will worship me, it will all be yours. (Luke 4:7)

Poem

(*This could be shared among several readers.*)

When Jesus was hungry, the Devil said,
'Turn these dry stones into bread.
There's no need to starve when with your power
you could grind these pebbles into flour.
Hear those hungry people cry;
are you so heartless as to let them die?
Think of the world in all its need;
what a saviour you'd be if you gave them bread.'

But Jesus looked in silence
to the far horizon
and saw . . .
you and me, in our complacency.
For we had learned
to turn stones into bread.
But we still had stony faces without joy
and stony hearts without love;
while the world was starving for justice.

So Jesus turned back to the Devil and said,
'I will not turn these stones into bread.
For everyone but you must own
that man shall not live by bread alone.
And the only thing that really feeds
is the Word that from God's mouth proceeds.'

Then the Devil tried a different tack
in order our Lord's will to crack.
He took him to a Temple tower
and showed him how to get great power:
by throwing himself from this high steeple
he would dazzle and amaze the people,
for angels just in time would fly
to hold him up lest he should die.

But Jesus looked in silence
to the far horizon
and saw . . .
you and me, in our credulity;
how we were blinded
by the glitter of our gods,
so that open-mouthed
we could see and believe
anything but the Truth
(which is invisible
and requires inner eyes).

So he turned to the Devil
and snapped his reply,
'It shall not be my way to lie,
and trick and smile and hypnotise
and wear a conjuror's disguise,
and use the gift of heavenly power
to gain men's praise for one brief hour.
What Scripture says is plain and best:
"You shall not put God to the test."'
But the Devil was not beaten yet;
he took Jesus from that parapet
to the top of a mountain where clouds unfurled,
revealing the kingdoms of the world.
'All that,' said the Devil, 'I'll give to you,
if you bow to me with worship true.'

But Jesus looked in silence
to the far horizon
and saw . . .
you and me, in our degeneracy,
bowing beneath the Devil's heavy load,
having received power to become
lords of the earth.

Then Jesus in anger,
in red-blooded anger,
cut the Devil down to size.
He glared at him with blazing eyes
and asked him who gave *him* the right
to dole out this world's wealth and might
and call on all the human race
to bow down low before his face.
For only one God reigns above;
him only should we serve and love.
'So, begone Satan!' Jesus cried,
'with your foul conspiracies I'll not side.'

Then angels came to help our Lord
with heavenly power to preach the Word,
and live a life of burning love
which all this aching world would move.

Peter Dainty, adapted

Second Sunday of Lent

Year A

Genesis 12:1-4a
Psalm 121
Romans 4:1-5, 13-17
John 3:1-17

So Abram went, as the Lord had told him. (Genesis 12:4a)

Prayer

Blessed are you, Lord our God,
for you have called us out of darkness
to be children of light.
The bright light of your presence
scatters the darkness within us
and is a guide on our journey.
Blessed are you, Father, Son and Holy Spirit.

We rejoice that in Christ we know
that light is stronger than darkness
and life is stronger than death.
Give your Church the courage
to proclaim the Good news to all people.
We remember all who are in doubt
or who are struggling with their faith.
We pray for those who have lost faith
and walk in darkness.

Lord, hear us:
come, lighten our darkness.

Amen.

David Adam

Poem

Abraham was called by God
to leave his home
among the nations
and to seek a better land –
a city that was built
on God's foundations.

So Abraham moved on,
not settling down
to die in Haran
like his father,
but shaking off the past
in searching for God's future.

Always travelling on,
he lived in tents,
a stranger and a refugee
even in Canaan.
He was to become
the father of all
those restless, wandering
and dissatisfied ones
who, like him, were haunted
by the persistent nudging
of the living God.

Abraham's descendants
are as countless as the stars –
pilgrims of the spirit,
and pioneers of faith,
whom God has chosen
to keep moving on,
until at last
they find their home
in God's eternal Kingdom.

Peter Dainty

Second Sunday of Lent

Year B

Genesis 17:1-7, 15, 16
Psalm 22:23-31
Romans 4:13-25
Mark 8:31-38

If any want to become my followers, let them deny themselves and take up their cross and follow me. (Mark 8:34)

Prayer

Blessed are you, Lord God.
You have called us into life,
to love and serve you.
You have promised that you are with us always
and that you are our Helper and our Guide.

We give thanks for all who hear and obey your call:
for men and women who willingly sacrifice
and deprive themselves for the good of others.
We remember all who have spent their lives in
 your service.
We ask you to give strength to all who are quietly
 seeking
to give you their love and their lives.
We remember today all who suffer rejection, pain
 or distress
for following you.

Lord, as you have called us,
hear us when we call upon you.
Amen.

David Adam

Poem

Good Jesus, who bore the cross for me, what cross is it you will that I should bear for you? You know, Lord, that I am all weakness; teach me to bear my cross: bear it for me, bear it in me.

Edward Pusey

Second Sunday of Lent

Year C

Genesis 15:1-12, 17, 18
Psalm 27
Philippians 3:17 – 4:1
Luke 13:31-35

Look towards heaven and count the stars, if you are able to count them
(Genesis 15:5)

Prayer

Gracious God,
so often we deny ourselves your blessing
through failing to turn to you;
failing to respond to your love
and to receive the mercy, joy, peace and new life
you so long to bring us.
We come now, therefore,
making time and space for you,
and opening our lives
to all you would pour into them.
Teach us, as we welcome you today,
to welcome you equally every day and every moment,
until you finally welcome us into your eternal kingdom,
through Jesus Christ our Lord.
Amen.

Nick Fawcett

Psalm 27

With God my Saviour as my light,
why should I be afraid?
The fiercest foes who threaten me
will find me undismayed.

God's temple is my chosen home;
his beauty draws my gaze –
though troubles rage on every side
my heart still flows with praise.

The focus of my prayer is this:
that I may see his face,
and prove his mercy more than plumbs
the depths of my disgrace.

And should my very family
acknowledge me no more,
the Lord remains my hiding-place –
in him I rest secure.

So when I find myself at risk
from lurking treachery,
Lord, show me how to walk with you
in full integrity.

For this I know: throughout my life
your love will hold me fast –
and I shall trust and hope in you
from this day to my last.

Martin E. Leckebusch

Metre: 86 86 (CM)
Suggested tune: *Westminster*

Third Sunday of Lent

Year A

Exodus 17:1-7
Psalm 95
Romans 5:1-11
John 4:5-42

Strike the rock, and water will come out of it, so that the people may drink.
(Exodus 17:6)

Prayer

God of all,
we thirst to know you better,
to grow closer to you each day.
Reach out now and speak your word of life.
Equip us to worship you in Spirit and in truth,
so that your grace may pour upon us,
and your love well up in our hearts,
refreshing, reviving and renewing,
satisfying body, mind and soul.
Meet us here, in all our weakness,
and grant us the living water
that you alone can give,
through Jesus Christ our Lord.
Amen.

Nick Fawcett

Poem

Dear Lord,
add my small drop
of prayer
to the cool cup of grace
you offer
this parched soul.
May he drink deep
and find himself
made whole.

Elizabeth Rooney

Third Sunday of Lent

Year B

Exodus 20:1-17
Psalm 19
1 Corinthians 1:18-25
John 2:13-22

He drove all of them out of the temple, both the sheep and the cattle. (John 2:15a)

Prayer

Lord Jesus Christ,
as you cleansed the temple in Jerusalem,
turning out everything that defiled it,
that prevented it from fulfilling its true purpose
and that separated rather than united people with
you,
so come now to our lives and cleanse our hearts,
removing in turn all that is unworthy,
that prevents us from being the people you would
have us be,
that destroys our relationship with you.
Re-create us,
making our bodies into a living temple,
honouring to you and filled by your presence,
so that we may truly worship you now
and faithfully serve you always,
by your grace.
Amen.

Nick Fawcett

Poem

Trust him
as if you were a daffodil
thrusting your vulnerable green
into the cold March air.
He has called you
to love and praise him here
in this strange modern scene.
He knows more than you know
about the pain
of being human
and the cost of sin.
He knows the wind is chill,
the snow half melted
and the ground still bare.
And yet, he calls like spring,
'Come, follow me!'
Be like the daffodils
and dare!

Elizabeth Rooney

Third Sunday of Lent

Year C

Isaiah 55:1-9
Psalm 63:1-9
1 Corinthians 10:1-13
Luke 13:1-9

A man had a fig tree planted in his vineyard; and he came looking for fruit on it and found none. (Luke 13:6)

Prayer

Lord God, our maker,
you are the source of all our life and strength,
the fountain of all that we know
and the provider of all that we need;
reach out to us in this act of worship,
that it may be more than a formal exercise of
religious tradition,
but rather, a means of grace.

Draw near to us, Lord:
that we may come closer to you.

Enlarge our understanding to take in some of
your greatness;
and make our minds sensitive to such light and
truth as we can bear.
Move us by your Spirit to respond to the mystery
of your presence.
Be our daily companion on the journey of life –
for you know the way we should go
and only your purposes are of lasting worth.

Draw near to us, Lord:
that we may come closer to you.

Forgive us when we seek after lesser things
and turn away from you and from our neighbours.
Make us aware of the needs of others
and of your glory in the world around us.
Disturb us with an inner restlessness
which will never be satisfied
until we become what you have made us to be.

Draw near to us, Lord:
that we may come closer to you.

Lord, hear our prayers,
and help us not only to speak but to listen,
and not only to listen, but to obey,
and not only to obey, but to love,
through Jesus Christ our Lord. Amen.

Peter Dainty

Psalm 63

Within my heart a desert lies –
an empty land, a barren place –
and like a traveller racked with thirst
I long for you, the God of grace.

Your power and glory once I knew:
those memories still enthral my mind –
they tell me that your presence brings
a feast for hungry souls to find.

When anxious thoughts disrupt my sleep,
to your unfailing care I cling
till, lifted by your tender strength,
my weary spirit starts to sing.

Whatever troubles lie ahead,
your constant love will see me through:
my God, my joy, I sing your praise –
my trust and triumph are in you.

Martin E. Leckebusch

Metre: 88 88 (LM)
Suggested tune: *Church Triumphant*

Fourth Sunday of Lent

Year A

1 Samuel 16:1-13
Psalm 23
Ephesians 5:8-14
John 9:1-41

He put mud on my eyes. Then I washed, and now I see. (John 9:15b)

Prayer

Gracious God,
open our eyes to your goodness, greatness, love and mercy,
for so often we fail to see as clearly as we should.
We close our eyes to what we would rather not face,
allow the concerns of each day
to obscure the wonder of your presence
or simply take for granted what has become so familiar.
Touch our lives now as we worship you,
and grant us, through all we share,
deeper insight,
a greater vision
and a clearer picture of who and what you are.
In Christ's name we pray.
Amen.

Nick Fawcett

Poem

Awake, you sleepers,
and rise from the dead,
and Christ will give you light.

Awake, you complacent dreamers,
mesmerised by the familiar merry-go-round;
easily persuaded that because today
is like yesterday,
tomorrow will be like today;
conditioned to receive
with drugged acceptance
the five immediate signals of the senses.
Must you sleep on
until the screen goes blank,
excited only by a sudden newsflash,
itself a part of your dream?
Wake now
to the more than sensible call of Christ.
Rise from your snug death bed
before you slide, blindfold, into hell.
Let Christ's stabbing light
reveal the nightmare reality
of your comfortable slumbers.
For it isn't true
that where there is no television
the people perish.
Awake, you sleep-walkers,
who yawn your aimless way
through a routine world,
treading the daily mill
with monotonous feet
which ache with boredom.
Throw off your stale shroud
and stretch your limbs and eyes
in the Eden freshness
of a Christ-filled dawn.

And you also,
who sleep the good sleep of faith –
like Christ in the stable
and the storm-shaken boat,
resting in God –
wake, like the wise maidens
with oil in their lamps
ready for midnight,
wake now to the bridegroom's calling,
inviting you
to the laughing, singing
wedding feast
of the new heaven
and the new earth.

Peter Dainty

Fourth Sunday of Lent

Year B

Numbers 21:4-9
Psalm 107:1-3, 17-22
Ephesians 2:1-10
John 3:14-21

Moses made a serpent of bronze, and put it upon a pole. (Numbers 21:9a)

Prayer

Gracious God,
remind us again as we worship you of how much
 you love us
and how much you are willing to do for our sakes.
Teach us to appreciate the full extent of your
 devotion
and to respond by consecrating our lives to Christ,
so that his grace may flow through us,
leading us out of darkness into his marvellous light.
Shine *upon* us,
within us
and *through* us,
for we ask it in his name.
Amen.

Nick Fawcett

Poem

Nicodemus thought
 that because Jesus did signs and wonders,
 he must be a man of God.
But Jesus knew
 that even the Devil does signs and wonders
 and deceives the world with them;
 but the true Man of God
 seeks only to do God's will.
And that is something the Devil can never do.

Nicodemus thought
 that the kingdom of God was a theocratic state
 that would be entered by triumphant processions
 of shouting zealots.
But Jesus knew
 that God's Kingdom cannot even be seen,
 let alone entered,
 except by those who have been reborn
 to a new kind of life.

Nicodemus thought
 that being born again
 meant re-entering his mother's womb.
 (Did he laugh when he said that?)
But Jesus knew
 that being born again meant, not baby bodies,
 but new hearts and minds,
 fashioned by the washing of repentance
 and the breathing of the Spirit.

'And the Son of Man,' said Jesus,
 'must be lifted up on a stick
 like Moses' serpent in the wilderness
 that everyone might see
 how much God loved the world,
 and seeing, live.'
We aren't told
 what Nicodemus made of that.
But was he any wiser,
when he came with spices
to lay the body of Jesus to rest
in the tomb?
And did he ever meet those
 who later found the tomb
 empty?

Do we too, like Nicodemus,
 misunderstand
 when Jesus speaks of heavenly things
 in the earthly language of metaphor and parable?
How, then, shall we ever understand him
 when he speaks the language of Heaven
 in a body raised from the dead?

Peter Dainty

Fourth Sunday of Lent

Year C

Joshua 5:9-12
Psalm 32
2 Corinthians 5:16-21
Luke 15:1-3, 11b-32

But while he was still far off, his father saw him and was filled with compassion. (Luke 15:20)

Prayer

Gracious God,
though we have repeatedly forgotten you –
going our own way,
squandering your blessing
and ignoring your will –
teach us that you long still to welcome us back,
your arms constantly outstretched to embrace us
once more.
In that faith we come now,
praising you for your goodness,
acknowledging our many faults,
thanking you for your mercy
and seeking to love and serve you better.
Receive us
and help us to open our hearts as wide to you
as yours is open to us.
Amen.

Nick Fawcett

Poem

Come to myself, I trudge down distant roads,
Tired of the husks of life, I hurry home.
Knowing the cross awaits, I still must come,
prepared to be a servant, not a son.

Your longing love outreaches me, outruns
my tardy progress borne on dragging feet.
Blessed, kissed, forgiven, lifted to my place,
I find the dreaded welcome sudden sweet.

Is this your punishment for sin, dear Lord?
The father's kiss? The ring? The robe? The calf?
Heart-heavy, I had feared repentance, Lord.
I came to cry, and now you tell me, 'Laugh!'

Elizabeth Rooney

Mothering Sunday

Years A, B & C

Exodus 2:1-10 or 1 Samuel 1:20-28
Psalm 34:11-20 or Psalm 127:1-4
2 Corinthians 1:3-7 or Colossians 3:12-17
Luke 2:33-35 or John 19:25b-27

She got a papyrus basket for him . . . she put the child in it and placed it among the reeds on the bank of the river. (Exodus 2:3)

Prayer

Caring and compassionate God,
speak to us today
through the love shown by mothers
of your love for us and all:
the love that brought us into being,
that has nurtured us across the years,
that welcomes us here
and that will go on reaching out,
come what may,
for all eternity.
Help us, as we honour what motherhood means,
to honour you also,
recognising that you show the same devotion and more,
an unswerving commitment to your children's welfare,
and teach us, as part of your family,
to respond accordingly,
loving you in return,
expressing our gratitude,
and living as you have taught us,
through Jesus Christ our Lord.
Amen.

Nick Fawcett

Poem

Lord of compassion, gracious and kind,
yours is a love which cares for us all;
Shepherd whose voice was known by your sheep,
still those who listen find that you call.
Hearing that call, we wonder indeed
why should you think us worth such a cost;
yet in our place you willingly died,
spending your life to rescue the lost.

Freedom you bring from all that enslaves;
worries you change for treasure untold;
and to the poor you offer a realm
where there are riches finer than gold.
Pardon us, Lord, that deep in our hearts
greed and injustice still we can find;
write on our lives your gracious concern
till we are loving, gentle and kind.

Tender your touch to soothe and restore:
healing you bring to body and soul.
Mighty in death, you conquered disease –
risen again, your life makes us whole.
Lord of compassion, right to the cross –
'Here is your son' and 'Father, forgive' –
teach us to walk your way on the earth;
work through us, Lord, as long as we live.

Martin E. Leckebusch

Fifth Sunday of Lent

Year A

Ezekiel 37:1-14
Psalm 130
Romans 8:6-11
John 11:1-45

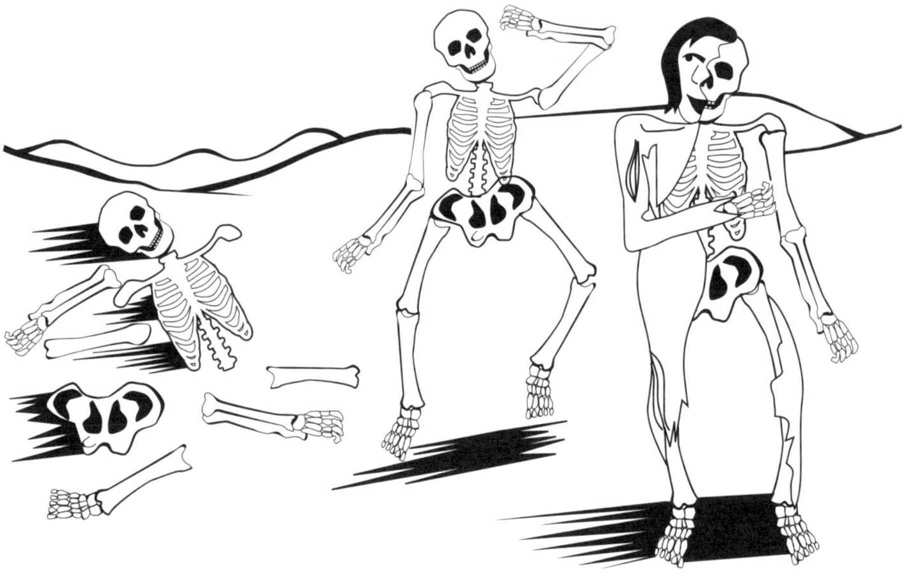

I will breath to enter you, and you shall live. (Ezekiel 37:5)

Prayer

Blessed are you, Lord our God,
who sent your Son to be our Saviour.
In your love you have opened for us
the way to eternal life
and rescued us from perishing.
Blessed are you, Father, Son and Holy Spirit.

Come, Lord, to refresh and renew your Church,
which without you is dull and dry.
Come fill the Church,
which without you is dead.
Fill the Church with your life-giving presence
and give it the power
to proclaim the resurrection to eternal life.
Lord, renew our faith in you.
Give to your Church a new sense of mission and
outreach.
Bless all preachers and ministers of the sacraments
with the joy of the Good News.

Come, Lord, revive us,
renew your people.

Amen.

David Adam

Poem (Psalm 130)

From the depths my soul cries out:
listen, Lord, to my plea;
on your mercy I depend –
hear my cry and answer me.

If you kept a list of sins
who could stand free of blame?
But forgiveness comes from you –
therefore I revere your name.

More than those who watch at night
for the coming of day –
more than this my eager soul
waits to hear what you will say.

Lord, may those who seek your love
find you faithful and true;
may your endless mercies reach
all who put their hope in you.

Martin E. Leckebusch

Fifth Sunday of Lent

Year B

Jeremiah 31:31-34
Psalm 51:1-13
  or Psalm 119:9-16
Hebrews 5:5-10
John 12:20-33

Very truly, I tell you, unless a grain of wheat falls into the earth and dies, it remains just a single grain; but if it dies, it bears much fruit. (John 12:24)

Prayer

Lord Jesus Christ,
speak to us of the new life you have made possible
through your stupendous sacrifice,
your willingness to surrender all.
Unfold to us the true nature of discipleship –
what it means to love and follow you –
and help us, by your grace, to respond,
dying to self and rising to new life with you,
so that all we do and are may be by our power,
in your service
and to your glory.
Amen.

Nick Fawcett

Poem

Where are the vows of long ago,
the promises I made,
the faith and trust I used to show,
the vision I displayed?
Where is the eagerness I knew
to follow day by day;
though others fail, to still stay true
and serve you come what may?
Where is the life I swore to lead,
the love I aimed to share,
the gentle word and thoughtful deed
that showed how much I care?
Lord, for all my lofty dreams
I've fallen so far short –
to walk the way of Christ, it seems,
is harder than I thought.
Make up in me the strength I lack
to stay true to your call,
for I would offer something back
to you who gave your all.

Nick Fawcett

Fifth Sunday of Lent

Year C

Isaiah 43:16-21
Psalm 126
Philippians 3:4b-14
John 12:1-8

The house was filled with the fragrance of the perfume. (John 12:3b)

Prayer

Lord of all,
fill us with love,
so that we might truly worship you.
May all we say, think and do come from the heart,
inspired by love in return,
and offered to you not because it's expected of us
but because we yearn to express our devotion,
to show you how much you mean to us
and how thankful we are
for the difference you've made to our lives.
Amen.

Nick Fawcett

Poem

I haven't cleaned the cellar,
I forgot to sweep the stair,
there's a button off my jacket,
Johnny's blue jeans have a tear,
there's an old arthritic lady
whom I should uphold in prayer,
and I'm sitting in the moonlight,
the moonlight, the moonlight,
adoring you by moonlight,
as if I had no care!

Elizabeth Rooney

Palm Sunday

Year A

Liturgy of the Palms
Matthew 21:1-11
Psalm 118:1, 2, 19-29

Liturgy of the Passion
Isaiah 50:4-9a
Psalm 31:9-16
Philippians 2:5-11
Matthew 26:14 – 27:66
or Matthew 27:11-54

Hosanna to the Son of David! (Matthew 21:9)

Prayer

Blessed are you, Lord God of our salvation;
to you be praise and glory for ever.
As we rejoice this day
in the triumphant entry into Jerusalem,
may we too be willing to walk the way of the cross.
By our lives may we witness to you as our Lord and King
and declare your saving love to the world.
Blessed are you, Father, Son and Holy Spirit.

Come, Lord.
Cleanse your Church from any pride or greed.
Cleanse us from our sins and free us to serve you.
Strengthen our sense of mission and service.
Strengthen our sensitivity towards the needs of others.
Strengthen our faith and our vision for your world.

Saviour of the world, our Redeemer,
save us and help us.

Amen. *David Adam*

Hymn

What kind of reign is this,
provoking such a scene?
These crowd, the palms, the cloaks, the songs:
what can they mean?
God's Chosen One arrives,
and loud hosannas ring
as on a donkey's foal he rides,
the humble King.

But with a heavy heart
this Prince of Peace has come,
his eyes awash with tears for lost
Jerusalem –
and in the temple courts
his holy anger burns:
the greedy money-changers' stalls
he overturns.

This promised, rightful Heir,
by prophets long foretold,
brings teaching and authority
both clear and bold;
the leaders whom he chides
respond with range and fear –
they plot his fate; the crisis grows;
the cross looms near.

They want his blood, he knows,
and he will be betrayed –
there in the darkened olive-grove
his choice is made:
he takes the bitter cup
with all it will entail,
resolved to face the agonies
of thorn and nail.

What kind of reign is this,
fulfilled at such a price:
a King who freely gives himself
in sacrifice!
With wonder we recall
the path our Saviour trod,
acknowledging the risen Christ
our Lord and God.

Martin E. Leckebusch

Metre: 6 6 8 4 D
Suggested tune: *Leoni*

Palm Sunday

Year B

Liturgy of the Palms
Mark 11:1-11
or John 12:12-16
Psalm 118: 1, 2, 19-24

Liturgy of the Passion
Isaiah 50:4-9a
Psalm 31:9-16
Philippians 2:5-11
Mark 14:1 – 15:47
or Mark 15:1-39 (40-47)

Take; this is my body. (Mark 14:22b)

Prayer

Blessed are you, Lord God of all creation.
You have created us out of your love and for your love.
Help us to welcome you with songs of 'Hosanna',
knowing that you are our strength and our shield.
Help us to welcome Christ our Lord into our lives
as our Lord and Saviour.

I will give thanks to you, for you answered me,
and have become my salvation.

Lord, by you we are wonderfully created.
Help us to use our talents and lives
to the benefit of others and to your glory.
May your Church be an instrument of peace in the world.
Lord, forgive the divisions of your Church
and help us to see we are one in you.
Help us to work together to bring in your kingdom.

I will give thanks to you, for you answered me,
and have become my salvation.

Amen.

David Adam

Hymn

On the night of his betrayal
when they were about to eat
Jesus knelt with towel and basin,
washing his disciples' feet.

On the night of his betrayal
special food had been prepared;
yet he brought a new fulfilment
to the ancient rite they shared.

On the night of his betrayal
taking wine and breaking bread,
he explained that he would suffer:
'This, my blood, for you is shed.'

On the night of his betrayal
Jesus had so much to say:
words to bring them reassurance
after he had gone away.

On the night of his betrayal
though aware of treachery,
still he chose to tread the pathway
into dark Gethsemane.

Martin E. Leckebusch

Metre: 8 7 8 7
Suggested tune: *Love Divine*

Palm Sunday

Year C

Liturgy of the Palms
Luke 19:28-40
Psalm 118:1, 2, 19-29

Liturgy of the Passion
Isaiah 50:4-9a
Psalm 31:9-16
Philippians 2:5-11
Luke 22:14 – 23:56
or Luke 23:1-49

Father, if you are willing, remove this cup from me; yet, not my will but yours be done. (Luke 22:42)

Prayer

Blessed are you, Lord our God, for you have redeemed us
by the offering of your Son upon the cross.
Through his death you destroy death
and open to us the kingdom of heaven.
As we seek to welcome Jesus into our lives
with cries of 'Hosanna',
and as we walk the way of the cross,
keep us ever mindful of your love and your peace.
Blessed are you, Father, with the Son and the Holy Spirit.
Amen.

David Adam

Poem

As you kneel there in the garden
in the coldness of the night,
and you contemplate the terror
of the quenching of the light,
do you think back to that garden –
and I speak now like a child –
to that perfect heaven, which was our home,
that Paradise undefiled,
and remember how you trembled
with your love for this poor earth,
as you emptied all your self
into that lowly stable birth:
the first step of a journey
through this world of sin and power,
on the path of loving service
which has brought you to this hour?
Do you remember how you left behind
that glorious world of light,
as you kneel there in the garden,
in the coldness of the night?

As you fall in prayer upon the grass
of dark Gethsemane,
are you thinking of that story
of the serpent and the tree?
Just a story known from childhood,
now rewritten in your life –
through the agony of temptation
and the sweat of inner strife.
As you ask if God is willing
to remove the cup of pain,
does the memory of Eden
steel your heart to think again,
and to bow before your calling
as the Father's loving Son,
and to say in calm acceptance:
'not my will, but yours, be done?'

Lord, we thank you for your courage
and we thank you for your love;
we have failed in our own Eden,
we're not fit for heaven above;
but we dare to claim the mercy
promised to the dying thief
as he cried out, 'Lord, remember me!'
in penitence and grief;
and you answered in your pity,
'Come with me to Paradise';
then submitted to the Father,
as you paid the sinner's price.

Peter Dainty

EASTER

Easter Day

Year A

Acts 10:34-43
or Jeremiah 31:1-6
Psalm 118:1, 2, 14-24
Colossians 3:1-4
or Acts 10:34-43
John 20:1-18
or Matthew 28:1-10

He is not here; for he has been raised, as he said. (Matthew 28:6a)

Prayer

Great and wonderful God,
today of all days we would praise you.
We would bring you our worship,
our gratitude, our faith
and our lives,
offering them to you in joyful celebration
at the victory you have won for us in Christ.
Grant, then, that everything we offer you today
will speak of our joy,
devotion
and desire to follow Christ;
to give ourselves to him as he gave himself for us.
Amen.

Nick Fawcett

Poem

Beware of stones;
they can be dangerous.

Some stones can trip,
and the unwary,
surprised in their carefree path
by unexpected stumbling blocks,
fall, and are broken.

Others, more careful,
walk around the stones,
but with eyes only for obstacles
they are blind
to a wider vision.

Others pick up their stones,
and strain beneath the weight
of guilt and fear,
grim Atlases,
bearing the world's burdens
on their neurotic shoulders.

But some kick stones,
like laughing schoolboys
oblivious of the risk, until,
too late, the damage has been done.

Or stones are thrown from angry fists
against the unyielding armour of authority,
or the stubborn heads of nonconformists,
or the easy target of the vulnerable,
or the innocent bystander.

Some bravely build with stones,
but their unsteady efforts
do not always stand the test
of quakes and storms.

Such are the various tricks
which we have learned
in handling stones,
and each one troublesome.

God has a better way –
his Easter morning angel came
and rolled away the stone
that blocked Christ's tomb;
and sat on it.

Peter Dainty

Easter Day

Year B

Acts 10:34-43
  or Isaiah 25:6-9
Psalm 118:1, 2, 14-24
1 Corinthians 15:1-11
  or Acts 10:34-43
John 20:1-18
  or Mark 16:1-8

Jesus said to her, 'Mary!'. (John 20:16a)

Prayer

Blessed are you, God and Father of us all,
giver of life and life eternal.
By the love of your Son you have triumphed over hatred.
In his power, light has conquered darkness
and life has overcome death.
You have opened for us the gate of eternal life.
Blessed are you, O God, now and for ever.

Lord, we are Easter People:
let 'Alleluia' be our song.

We give you thanks and praise
for the resurrection of our Lord Jesus Christ
and for his appearances to his loved ones.
We rejoice with the whole Church in the joy of the risen Lord.
May we who know the Good News
go and tell others that he is risen.
Grant that your Church may help to bring peace and hope
to a troubled world.
We ask you to give courage to all who have not seen
and yet believe.

Lord, we are Easter People:
let 'Alleluia' be our song.

Amen.

David Adam

Poem

Now is the shining fabric of our day
torn open, flung apart,
rent wide by Love.
Never again
the tight, enclosing sky,
the blue bowl,
or the star-illumined tent.
We are laid open to infinity,
for Easter Love
has burst his tomb and ours.
Now nothing shelters us
from God's desire –
not flesh, not sky,
not stars, not even sin.
Now Glory waits
so he can enter in.
Now does the dance begin.

Elizabeth Rooney

Easter Day

Year C

Acts 10:34-43
or Isaiah 65:17-25
Psalm 118:1, 2, 14-24
1 Corinthians 15:19-26
or Acts 10:34-43
John 20:1-18
or Luke 24:1-12

They did not believe them. (Luke 24:11)

Prayer

Lord of heaven and earth, we praise you
that having sent your Son into this world
to love and suffer and die for the sake of all humankind,
you raised him from the tomb in triumph over the darkness of death.

Praise be to God: **that Christ is alive!**

We thank you for those moving stories of the events of that first Easter Day –
the empty tomb and the mysterious appearances of the risen Christ,
reviving his disheartened friends with fresh faith, hope and courage.

Praise be to God: **that Christ is alive!**

We thank you for two thousand years of Christian history
in which the Church has not only remembered the Jesus of the past,
but experienced his living presence.

Praise be to God: **that Christ is alive!**

Help us also to share in the fellowship of his resurrection
and be revived in heart and mind by his energising Spirit.

Praise be to God: **that Christ is alive!**

Lord, we cannot fathom the mystery of your purposes,
but sometimes our spiritual eyes are opened
and by faith we know your holy presence.
You are greater than we can comprehend,
and yet you live within our hearts and minds.
We say you are in heaven,
and yet wherever we go on earth you are by our side.
Your goodness stands in judgement over our sinful lives,
and yet you come to offer us peace,
and welcome us, just as we are, into your Kingdom.

Praise be to God: **that Christ is alive!**

Lord, your ways are more amazing than even our boldest thoughts,
deeper than our wisest understanding
and more surprising than our largest expectations.
We thank you that in the death and resurrection of Jesus Christ
you have shown us that suffering love is a powerful instrument for good,
and that the grave can be the gateway to eternal life.

Praise be to God: **that Christ is alive!**

So then we rejoice on this Easter morning
and add our feeble alleluias
to the chorus of your Church throughout the world
and the greater music of the saints in heaven.
For Christ is risen! **He is risen indeed!** Alleluia!
Amen!

Peter Dainty

Poem

The Love I love,
came in the early dawning,
standing as still as light.

How could I ever have dreamed
so sweet a morning
after so dark a night?

Elizabeth Rooney

Second Sunday of Easter

Year A

Acts 2:14a, 22-32
Psalm 16
1 Peter 1:3-9
John 20:19-31

My Lord and my God! (John 20:28)

Prayer

Blessed are you,
God and Father of our Lord Jesus Christ.
To you be glory and praise for ever.
By raising your Son from the dead,
death has been destroyed
and new life has been restored.
In him the victory over sin and the grave is won.
As you call us to newness of life,
may our lives reflect his glory.
Blessed are you, Father, Son and Holy Spirit.

Lord, bless your Church,
that it may reveal your presence
and the power of the resurrection.
May each church community
show signs of new life and joy in you.
Through our relationship with you
may we bring others to be faithful.
We ask your blessing upon all who are seekers,
all who are new in the faith
and all who are struggling
with doubt and darkness.

Lord, be known among us;
make haste to help us.

Amen.

David Adam

Poem

If you choose doubting Thomas
as your patron saint,
simply because, like you,
he would only believe
the things he could touch or see,
do not then rest
in agnostic security.
But remember that, in the end,
even Thomas was convinced
by the unexpected evidence of his senses.
And Christ may yet turn
even *your* doubt into faith,
by showing you his wounds.

Peter Dainty

Second Sunday of Easter

Year B

Acts 4:32-35
Psalm 133
1 John 1:1 – 2:2
John 20:19-31

God is light and in him there is no darkness at all. (1 John 1:5b)

Prayer

Lord of Light, in whom there is no darkness at all,
we praise you for the morning,
when light triumphs over darkness.

We praise you for the light of beauty,
shining in your creation.

We praise you for the light of goodness,
shining in the lives of those who love you
and have learned to love their neighbours as
themselves.

We praise you for the light of joy,
reflected in the singing of angels
and the worship of your people here on earth.

Forgive us that we do not always live in your light,
but in the shadows of our self-concern.

Forgive us when there has been darkness
in our thoughts and feelings,
our words and actions;
when we have been irritable and moody,
and made others miserable
by the thoughtless and hurtful things we have
said or done.

We thank you for those whose light has shone
into our darkness
and shown us a better way;
for those who have loved us when we haven't
deserved it,
who have been patient with us in our faults,
who have been generous to us in our self-
centredness.

We thank you for those whose genuine goodness
has inspired and helped us,
whose courage in adversity has amazed us,
whose dedication to the truth has deeply moved us.
For through them your love has lit up our lives
with faith and hope.

We thank you for Jesus, the light of the world;
may his light be reflected even in us
by the miracle of your grace.

We ask this in his name. Amen.

Peter Dainty

Poem

Make me
a still place of light
a still place of love
of you
your light radiating
your love vibrating
your touch and your healing
far flung and near
to the myriads caught
in darkness, in sickness
in lostness, in fear

make a heart-centre here,
Light of the world.

Malling Abbey

Second Sunday of Easter

Year C

Acts 5:27-32
Psalm 118:14-29
or Psalm 150
Revelation 1:4-8
John 20:19-31

This is the gate of the Lord; the righteous shall enter through it.
(Psalm 118:20)

Prayer

Blessed are you, God and Father of our Lord Jesus Christ.
To you be praise and glory for ever.
Alleluia.
By the raising of your Son from the dead
you have opened to us the way to eternal life.
You have given us an everlasting joy and a deep peace
through bringing us to know the risen Christ.
Blessed are you, Father, Son and Holy Spirit.

Risen Christ, be known among us
and give us your peace.

Amen.

David Adam

Poem

Give glory to Jesus
whose rising from the dead
surpasses fulfilment
of all the prophets said:
from days of old
their words foretold
his anguish and his reign –
he died, and rose again,
so praise the Living Lord!

Give glory to Jesus
who lives for evermore,
by whose vindication
we know we stand secure:
our debt is cleared,
and all we feared
now shrivels in the light
of love's triumphant might –
so praise the Living Lord!

Give glory to Jesus
who reigns as gracious Lord,
transforming the future
through broken lives restored:
from hearts ablaze
with love and praise
we yearn to do his will –
so now with all our skill
we praise our Living Lord!

Martin E. Leckebusch

Third Sunday of Easter

Year A

Acts 2:14a, 36-41
Psalm 116:1-3, 10-17
1 Peter 1:17-23
Luke 24:13-35

Jesus himself came near and went with them. (Luke 24:15)

Prayer

Lord Jesus Christ,
as those who walked with you on the Emmaus Road
recognised you in the breaking of bread,
so may we recognise you now as we join in worship.
Grant that we too may meet with you,
walk with you
and talk with you,
so that our hearts might burn within us
as we go on our way, rejoicing.
Open our hearts, today and every day,
to your living presence and life-giving power.
Amen.

Nick Fawcett

Poem

(*For two readers, representing the two disciples.*)

Cleopas: As we walked along the road
with the sunset in our eyes,
all the world seemed turned to blood
by the redness of the skies.

2nd disciple: And our voices were low,
and our footsteps were slow,
we had nowhere to go
tomorrow.

Cleopas: As we walked along the road
we were talking of the cross,
when a stranger heard our sighs
but knew nothing of our loss.

2nd disciple: How the master was dead
who had offered us bread;
now we only knew dread
and sorrow.

Cleopas: As we walked along the road
he began to speak with power
of the hidden things of God
which were destined for this hour.

2nd disciple: And he raised our hope higher,
filled our hearts with strange fire
and rekindled our desire
for living.

Cleopas: When we reached our resting place
we persuaded him to stay,
(though he made as if to go
further on the dusty way).

2nd disciple: And the words that he said
as he gave us the bread
made us sure that the dead
was living.

Cleopas: We ran back along the road,
though the stars were in the skies,
ran to tell what we had seen
when the scales fell from our eyes.

Both: And we sang a new song,
as we bounded along,
of the Lord who was strong
and living.

Peter Dainty

Third Sunday of Easter

Year B

Acts 3:12-19
Psalm 4
1 John 3:1-7
Luke 24:36b-48

Jesus himself stood among them and said to them, 'Peace be with you'.
(Luke 24:36)

Prayer

Blessed are you, mighty God,
creator of light and darkness.
To you be praise and glory for ever.
By the resurrection of your Son to eternal life
you have destroyed the darkness and fear of death.
Radiant life is ours through him who loves us,
Jesus, our Lord and our Friend.
Blessed are you, Father, Son and Holy Spirit,
our God for ever and ever.
Amen.

David Adam

Poem

There comes a moment
when we lay aside
life's winding sheets
and, springing from the tomb,
of flesh, time, space,
go forth
to meet our Lover
face to face.

Elizabeth Rooney

Third Sunday of Easter

Year C

Acts 9:1-6 (7-20)
Psalm 30
Revelation 5:11-14
John 21:1-19

Jesus said to them, 'Come and have breakfast'. (John 21:12a)

Prayer

Blessed are you, Lord our God,
for you have called us out of darkness
into the glorious light of your presence;
you fill our emptiness with the richness of your love.
We rejoice in the power of the resurrection
and in your gift of eternal life.
Blessed are you, Father, Son and Holy Spirit.

Lord, we thank you for calling us to follow you
and to share in your outreach to all peoples.
We ask your blessing upon all who go out to
preach the word,
upon all pastors and shepherds of your flock.
Give us all the wisdom to follow in your steps
and to bring others to know and love you.
We pray for all who are involved in mission
and in spreading the Good News
through teaching and example.

Hear us, O Lord, and have mercy upon us;
O Lord, be our helper.
Amen.

David Adam

Hymn

You stood there on the shoreline
and waited in the dawn
to share with your disciples
the newness of the morn;
be with us now, Lord Jesus,
and make your presence known:
in resurrection power
declare today your own.

When hours of tiring labour
had brought them scant reward,
in your immense provision
they recognised their Lord;
when drudgery seems endless,
demeaning all our skill,
let this be our contentment:
to know and do your will.

On bread and fish they feasted
around a charcoal fire:
that resurrection breakfast
was all they could desire!
Like them, may we discover
the joy which never ends
when you, the King of glory,
count us among your friends.

Where Simon Peter languished
in guilt and burning shame,
you spoke of restoration,
and not of endless blame;
where sin and failure haunt us,
remind us what is true:
that we are now forgiven
and called to follow you.

Martin E. Leckebusch

Metre: 7 6 7 6 D
Suggested tunes: *Thornbury; Wolvercote*

Fourth Sunday of Easter

Year A

Acts 2:42-47
Psalm 23
1 Peter 2:19-25
John 10:1-10

He calls his own sheep by name and leads them out. (John 10:3b)

Prayer

O God, whose Son Jesus Christ is the good shepherd of your people: grant that when we hear his voice we may know him who calls us each by name, and follow where he leads; who, with you and the Holy Spirit, lives and reigns, one God, for ever and ever.

Episcopal Church, USA

Poem

Lord of compassion, gracious and kind,
yours is a love which cares for us all;
Shepherd whose voice was known by your sheep,
still those who listen find that you call.
  Hearing that call, we wonder indeed
  why should you think us worth such a cost;
  yet in our place you willingly died,
  spending your life to rescue the lost.

Freedom you bring from all that enslaves;
worries you change for treasure untold;
and to the poor you offer a realm
where there are riches finer than gold.
  Pardon us, Lord, that deep in our hearts
  greed and injustice still we can find;
  write on our lives your gracious concern
  till we are loving, gentle and kind.

Tender your touch to soothe and restore:
healing you bring to body and soul.
Mighty in death, you conquered disease –
risen again, your life makes us whole.
  Lord of compassion, right to the cross –
  'Here is your son' and 'Father, forgive' –
  teach us to walk your way on the earth;
  work through us, Lord, as long as we live.

Martin E. Leckebusch

Fourth Sunday of Easter

Year B

Acts 4:5-12
Psalm 23
1 John 3:16-24
John 10:11-18

I am the good shepherd. (John 10:11a)

Prayer

Lord Jesus Christ,
shepherd of the sheep,
Lamb of God,
we thank you that though we repeatedly err and stray,
ignoring your voice and wandering far from your side,
you not only seek us out,
but also willingly lay down your life for us,
freely giving that we might freely receive.
Equip us now to show our gratitude by following you more closely,
trusting you more completely
and obeying you more faithfully,
so that our lives as well as our words may give honour to you,
now and always.
Amen.

Nick Fawcett

Poem

Shepherd, my shepherd,
far have I strayed,
lost to your love for me,
hurt and betrayed –
and yet your love comes seeking.

Shepherd, my shepherd,
I've been alone,
bruising myself
on the shale and stone –
and still your love comes seeking.

Shepherd, my shepherd,
I've torn my fleece,
caught in life's brambles,
lost to your peace –
and now your love comes finding.

Shepherd, my shepherd,
I'm in your arms,
safe from myself
and from evil's alarms –
and with your love comes healing.

Elizabeth Rooney

Fourth Sunday of Easter

Year C

Acts 9:36-43
Psalm 23
Revelation 7:9-17
John 10:22-30

My sheep hear my voice. I know them, and they follow me. (John 10:27)

Prayer

Praise to you, O faithful God!
You never fail those who trust in you,
but you allow them to share in your glory.
You fight for us against everything
that could attack or do us harm.
You are our shepherd,
and you free us from the snare.
You protect us who honour you, O God;
great is the sweetness that you give.

Notker

Hymn

When circumstances make my life
too hard to understand,
no doubt or fear, no pain or strife,
can snatch me from God's hand.

In valleys where the path is steep,
with shadows dark and long,
I know the Shepherd leads his sheep –
his grace will keep me strong.

Though sorrow and perplexity
are often what I feel,
Gethsemane and Calvary
affirm God's love is real.

It is enough for me to know
his promise and his care:
wherever on life's path I go
my Saviour will be there.

Martin E. Leckebusch

Metre: 8 6 8 6 (CM)
Suggested tunes: *Contemplation; St Bernard*

Fifth Sunday of Easter

Year A

Acts 7:55-60
Psalm 31:1-5, 15, 16
1 Peter 2:2-10
John 14:1-14

I am the way, and the truth, and the life. No one comes to the Father except through me. (John 14:6)

Prayer

We thank you, Lord, for this amazing journey of life, this pilgrimage through time, which is so full of the unexpected. We thank you that we do not travel alone, but we have each other with whom to share both the joys and the sorrows. And you are with us to guide, to support, to encourage and to strengthen on the way. Lord, help us to know that in all the circumstances of our lives you are the Good Shepherd who walks with us.

When we are weak and weary,
make us to lie down in green pastures.
When we are anxious and afraid,
lead us beside still waters and restore our souls.
When we are confused and lost, show us the way.
When, in our busyness, we forget you, and
  wander away,
do not forget us, but come and seek us out.
When, in our foolishness and selfishness, we are
  tempted to go astray,
bring us back to the right path.
When we face the valley of shadows, be with us to
  bring us safely through.
On every step of our pilgrimage through life and
  death
help us to put our trust in you, our sure and
  loving shepherd, companion and friend,
through Jesus Christ our Lord. Amen.

Peter Dainty

Poem

Must you be always trudging,
merely trudging?
Can you not hear the silver trumpets call?
These years are meant for blessing.
Don't go grudging
along the road decreed for you above.
Rather with high and happy heart,
with singing,
with banners flying
go upon your way.
Know in your heart
that every step is bringing
you closer
to that final glorious day!

Elizabeth Rooney

Fifth Sunday of Easter

Year B

Acts 8:26-40
Psalm 22:25-31
1 John 4:7-21
John 15:1-8

I am the vine, you are the branches. (John 15:5a)

Prayer

Lord Jesus Christ,
teach us to honour you
not just through songs of worship,
words of prayer
or the outward practice of religion,
but also through lives rooted in you,
entwined with yours
and producing fruits of the Spirit,
our love, joy, peace and humility speaking to
    others of you.
Dwell in us
and unite us with you,
that we may truly glorify your name,
here;
and everywhere.
Amen.

Nick Fawcett

Psalm 23

Within the busy rush of life
    I find a resting-place:
when I submit to Christ my Lord
    and let him set my pace
he shows the way that I should take
    whatever trials I face.

Amid the choices I must make
    and duties that increase
he comes to calm my anxious thoughts,
    to make the turmoil cease;
as in his presence I remain
    he guides me into peace.

The timeless, all-sufficient God
    my every longing knows
and daily he refreshes me
    with joy which overflows;
anointed by tranquillity
    my strength to serve him grows.

My Saviour bids me walk with him
    and follow all his ways –
his plan for me is fruitfulness
    throughout my earthly day,
since now and evermore I live
    beneath his loving gaze.

Martin E. Leckebusch

Metre: 8 6 8 6 8 6
Suggested tune: *Brother James' Air*

Fifth Sunday of Easter

Year C

Acts 11:1-18
Psalm 148
Revelation 21:1-6
John 13:31-35

I give you a new commandment, that you love one another. (John 13:34a)

Prayer

Lord Jesus Christ,
we come to you in worship,
seeking to learn more of you
and to welcome you more fully into our lives.
We come,
yearning to love as you have loved us –
to show the truth of our faith
and the authenticity of our discipleship
through our devotion to one another and to you,
and through our concern for others.
Help us, through this service,
to recognise the ways in which we fall short of
that calling,
to acknowledge these honestly to you,
and to open our hearts afresh to your face,
so that your love might grow within us
and overflow to your praise and glory.
Amen.

Nick Fawcett

Poem

I try so hard to love, Lord,
to reach out in your name;
to know the worst in people
but cherish them the same.
I strive to show compassion,
to show I really care –
yet measured by your goodness
such love cannot compare.
For what I give is partial,
a prize that must be earned;
its constancy dependent
on whether it's returned.
The love you give, in contrast,
is free and unreserved;
poured out with no restrictions,
although it's undeserved.
Lord, come and work within me,
transform my heart of stone,
until the love I offer
grows closer to your own.

Nick Fawcett

Sixth Sunday of Easter

Year A

Acts 17:22-31
Psalm 66:7-18
1 Peter 3:13-22
John 14:15-21

He has kept us among the living, and has not let our feet slip. (Psalm 66:9)

Prayer

Loving God,
we want to worship you, not just now but always –
through faithful discipleship
and obedience to your will,
through lives of love pleasing in your sight –
but we cannot do it by ourselves:
we need your help.
Draw near through your Spirit of truth,
and, through the power of the risen Christ,
transform, re-create and make us new,
so that we may praise you now and honour you
always,
to the glory of your name.
Amen.

Nick Fawcett

Poem

When I'm feeling low,
nowhere left to go,
always, Lord, you show
you are there, every step that I go.

When I'm in despair,
spirit crushed by care,
life too hard to bear,
you are there – every step, everywhere.

When my dreams have died,
hopes have been denied,
nowhere left to hide,
still you're there, every step by my side.

When I feed a friend
aching wounds to tend,
broken heart to mend,
you are there, every step to the end.

Every single day,
by my side you stay,
with me, come what may,
always there, every step of the way.

Nick Fawcett

Sixth Sunday of Easter

Year B

Acts 10:44-48
Psalm 98
1 John 5:1-6
John 15:9-17

Make a joyful noise to the Lord, all the earth. (Psalm 98:4)

Prayer

Living Lord,
as we celebrate your resurrection,
help us also to keep in mind what made it possible:
your readiness to endure the agony and anguish
of the cross;
your love so great
that you were willing to lay down your life for our
sake.
Write that truth once more in our hearts today,
so that the worship we offer now
will be reinforced by the love we show in turn,
to you,
to each other
and to all.
In your name we pray.
Amen.

Nick Fawcett

Psalm 98

Come with newly-written anthems,
craft your finest psalm or song;
praise the God of marvellous mercy,
our deliverer, swift and strong –
he reveals his holy kindness
so that all the world may know:
never once has he forgotten
what he promised long ago.

Bring your hymns of celebration;
be creative, and rejoice;
blend as one your skilful playing,
thankful heart and cheerful voice.
Let the wonders of God's greatness
be your focus as you sing;
weaving reverence and excitement,
raise the shout: the Lord is King!

Sing until the whole creation
echoes to the melody,
till the seas and hills and rivers
join the swelling symphony:
for he comes, and every nation
shall receive its just reward –
sing to greet the God of justice,
righteous Judge and gracious Lord.

Martin E. Leckebusch

Metre: 87 87 D
Suggested tunes: *Ode to Joy; Bethany*

Sixth Sunday of Easter

Year C

Acts 16:9-15
Psalm 67
Revelation 21:10, 22–22:5
John 14:23-29
  or John 5:1-9

Jesus said to him, 'Stand up, take your mat and walk'. (John 5:8)

Prayer

Sovereign God,
come *among* us,
upon us
and *within* us
through your Holy Spirit,
so that we might be equipped both to know your will and to do it.
Grant us an inner experience of your presence,
so that your word might be unfolded,
your peace given,
your love nurtured
and your power imparted,
such that we might honour you
not just here and now
but in every place and at all times,
through keeping your commands
and observing your will.
In Christ's name we pray.
Amen.

Nick Fawcett

Poem

I was once content
just staring at the waters,
sitting by the edge of the pool;
waiting for an angel
to stir up the water,
sitting by the edge of the pool.

But Jesus came
with a word that pierced my heart;
he asked me a question
that tore my soul apart:
'Do you want to be whole?'
Did I really, really want to be whole?

I was once resigned
to a life without a purpose,
sitting by the edge of the pool;
with a paralysed mind
that didn't want a purpose,
sitting by the edge of the pool.

Then Jesus came
and he got me off my seat;
he challenged me to stand
on my own two feet:
'Pick up your mat and walk,' he said,
and I did, yes I did!
And I knew, within my soul,
that this Jesus had made me whole!

Peter Dainty

Ascension Day

Years A, B & C

Acts 1:1-11
  or Daniel 7:9-14
Psalm 47
  or Psalm 93
Ephesians 1:15-23
  or Acts 1:1-11
Luke 24:44-53

(The reading from Acts must be one of the readings for the day.)

He was lifted up, and a cloud took him out of their sight. (Acts 1:9)

Prayer

Blessed are you, Lord our God,
for in the ascension of your Son
you have raised us on high
and given us a glimpse of eternal life
and the promise of your abiding presence.
Blessed are you, Father, Son and Holy Spirit.

Risen and ascended Lord,
you have promised to be with us always.
Help us to rejoice in your presence
and to proclaim your saving power.
We ask your blessing upon all who preach the
  Good News,
all who teach from the Scriptures
and all who witness to you in their daily lives.

Ascended Lord, King of kings,
rule in our hearts and in the world.
Amen.

David Adam

Poem

Shall we gaze into the sky,
waiting for the coming of the Christ
who never left us?
Do we look to the heavens
for the one who lives in our hearts?
Has he left the stage
of the world's drama
in order to return in triumph
and save us all
just in time?

Or will the flash of his appearing
strike upon our vision
not from the clouds above,
but from the depths of faith and love
in those who already see him?

Peter Dainty

Seventh Sunday of Easter

Year A

Acts 1:6-14
Psalm 68:1-10, 32-35
1 Peter 4:12-14; 5:6-11
John 17:1-11

Father, the hour has come; glorify your Son so that the Son may glorify you.
(John 17:1b)

Prayer

Blessed are you, Lord our God,
for you have raised your Son
from the darkness of death
to the fullness of life eternal,
to your right hand on high.
By his death he has destroyed death;
by his rising to life again
he has restored to us eternal life;
by his ascension
he has opened for us the gate of glory.
Blessed are you, Father, Son and Holy Spirit.

As we rejoice in the ascension,
we give thanks for men and women of vision,
for those who have shared their faith with us.
We remember all whose lives are clouded by
doubt or despair.
We pray for those who feel life is dull,
that they may come to know
the joy of the presence of the ascended Lord.
Lord, empower your Church
to proclaim the Good News of your saving acts.

Lord, with us always,
hear us and help us.
Amen.

David Adam

Hymn

Christ our Lord, we worship you,
for you left eternal glory,
taking mortal flesh and blood,
born to share our human story;
hallelujah!

Some who climbed a mountain high
glimpsed the truth – and fell, dumbfounded:
was your honour not disclosed
when the Father's voice resounded?
Hallelujah!

Yet a greater glory shone
when you faced humiliation,
when you suffered in our place,
crucified for our salvation;
hallelujah!

And your resurrection proved
sin's oppressive grasp was ended,
for you rose as living Lord
and in triumph you ascended;
hallelujah!

What a hope we now possess,
far surpassing earthly measure
for your Spirit thrills our hearts
with a taste of heaven's treasure!
Hallelujah!

When in splendour you return
every knee shall bow before you!
Come, our King, and take your throne –
hallelujah! We adore you!
Hallelujah!

Martin E. Leckebusch

Metre: 7 8 7 8 4
Suggested tune: *St Albinus*

Seventh Sunday of Easter

Year B

Acts 1:15-17, 21-26
Psalm 1
1 John 5:9-13
John 17:6-19

And they cast lots for them, and the lot fell on Matthias. (Acts 1:26a)

Prayer

Blessed are you, Lord our God.
You are always with us
and ready to hear our prayers.
You have called us by our name
and wait for us to turn to you.
You have chosen us to work with you
and you seek to fill us with your Spirit.
Blessed are you, Father, Son and Holy Spirit.

We give you thanks for men and women of prayer
who have revealed your love
and helped us to know of your presence.
We remember before you
all who are evangelists and ministers,
all who proclaim your love for us.
May we share in the ministry and the outreach
of your Church.

Lord, as we wait upon you,
hear our prayer.
Amen.

David Adam

Hymn

Called by Christ to be disciples
every day in every place,
we are not to hide as hermits
but to spread the way of grace;
citizens of heaven's kingdom,
though this world is where we live,
as we serve a faithful Master,
faithful service may we give.

Richly varied are our pathways,
many callings we pursue:
may we use our gifts and talents
always, Lord, to honour you;
so in government or commerce,
college, hospice, farm or home,
whether volunteers or earning,
may we see your kingdom come.

Hard decisions may confront us,
urging us to compromise;
still obedience is our watchword –
Father, make us strong and wise!
Secular is turned to sacred,
made a precious offering,
as our daily lives are fashioned
in submission to our King.

Martin E. Leckebusch

Metre: 8 7 8 7 D
Suggested tunes: *Hyfrydol; Alleluia*

Seventh Sunday of Easter

Year C

Acts 16:16-34
Psalm 97
Revelation 22:12-14, 16, 17, 20, 21
John 17:20-26

Sirs, what must I do to be saved? (Acts 16:30)

Prayer

Gracious God,
open our hearts afresh today
to the fullness of life you want us to experience,
not only in eternity but also here and now –
life lived in union with you,
in harmony with your will
and in the light of your love.
Draw us closer to your side,
so that whatever separates us from you,
undermining the unity you want us to enjoy,
will be overcome,
our lives in consequence bearing witness to you,
so that others in turn
might know and believe in you for themselves,
through Jesus Christ our Lord,
Amen.

Nick Fawcett

Poem

You've called us as your Church, Lord,
your people here on earth,
a fellowship of equals
where all are given worth,
a family together,
distinguished by our care,
one faith, one hope, one gospel,
one vision that we share.
Yet we have been divided
by doctrine, dogma, creed,
estranged from one another –
we've left your wounds to bleed.
Too full of our convictions,
believing others wrong,
we've lost sight of the body
to which we all belong.
Our differences deny you,
betray the faith we claim;
instead of love uniting,
we squabble in your name.
Lord, heal the wounds that scar us –
suspicion, fear and pride;
reveal the good in others
that all our labels hide.
May cords of love unite us,
too strong to be undone –
although we may be many,
equip us to be one.

Nick Fawcett

Pentecost

(Whit Sunday)

Year A

Acts 2:1-21
  or Numbers 11:24-30
Psalm 104:24-34, 35b
1 Corinthians 12:3b-13
  or Acts 2:1-21
John 20:19-23
  or John 7:37-39

(The reading from Acts must be used as the first or second reading.)

Now there are varieties of gifts, but the same Spirit. (1 Corinthians 12:4)

Prayer

Lord, we greet you, on this the birthday of your Church. We thank you for the gift of your Spirit, poured out upon those first disciples long ago, and present with all who have followed them since in faith and obedience to your way.

Holy Spirit of God, we praise you that you are present with us in worship and prayer, as you have been present with your people in all ages – around us, among us and within us.

Holy Spirit of God: **fill your Church today.**

We praise you for your divine energy, ever active in the world, from the first day of creation until now, inspiring prophets and saints in every generation, and guiding your people in their mission and earthly pilgrimage.

So guide and direct our lives, and the life of your Church, today and in the days to come. May we discover your gifts among us for the building up of the Church – gifts of witness, service, teaching, helpfulness and pastoral care.

Holy Spirit of God: **fill your Church today.**

When the Church seeks power,
show us the way of service.
When the Church abuses its wealth,
show us the meaning of sacrifice and generosity.
When the Church is wrapped up in its rituals,
teach us the secret of simplicity.
When the Church teaches fashionable opinions,
correct us with the truth of your eternal Word.
When the Church becomes apathetic, fearful or
  pessimistic
give us faith, hope and love.

Holy Spirit of God: **fill your Church today.**

Forgive us when we quench your work by our apathy, self-interest or lack of faith, and help us to make room for you to bear rich fruit in our lives – the fruit of love, joy, peace, patience, kindness, goodness, faithfulness, gentleness and self-control.

Spirit of truth fill our minds,
Spirit of Christ, fill our hearts,
Spirit of power and holiness, revive your Church,
Spirit of love bind us together in Christian
  fellowship,
Spirit of justice and peace, lead all nations into
  your Kingdom,

Holy Spirit of God: **fill your Church today.**

In the name of Jesus. Amen.

Peter Dainty

Poem

Once, very quietly, Love came
as baby, innocent and mild.
But we? We killed the Holy Child.
Then was Love true to Love.
For all that we could do,
he stayed the same.
He did not hate us for his death.
Again, he came –
this time
as living breath of flame.

Elizabeth Rooney

Pentecost

(Whit Sunday)

Year B

Acts 2:1-21
or Ezekiel 37:1-14
Psalm 104:24-34, 35b
Romans 8:22-27
or Acts 2:1-21
John 15:26, 27; 16:4b-15

And suddenly from heaven there came a sound like the rush of a violent wind.
(Acts 2:2)

Prayer

Blessed are you, Lord our God.
Your Spirit comes to our weakness with his power.
In the strength of your Spirit
you enable us to live and work
to your praise and glory.
May we who have received the gifts of the Spirit
use them for the benefit of your creation
and to reveal your love in the world.
Blessed are you, Lord God,
Father, Son and Holy Spirit.

Lord, as we rejoice in the coming of the Spirit
we give thanks for all who proclaim
your presence and power.
We remember all preachers and evangelists,
all who celebrate the sacraments and minister to us.
May all your people share fully
in forwarding the Gospel and revealing your love.

We rejoice that you fill our world.
Your Spirit is with us.
Amen.

David Adam

Poem

The Spirit is a lively wind –
breathtaking
for those who breathe
the stale air of mechanical worship;
but for sails unfurled
and wings of faith spread wide
he comes as driving energy,
uncontrollably bracing.
He only destroys cobwebs
and dead branches.

The Spirit is a lively power –
not available
to bolster up our empires,
but unpredictably exploding
in surprising places,
strengthening weak knees
and faint hearts,
and giving secret growth
to mysterious fruit.
He only destroys
the rotten enemies
of our souls.

The Spirit is a lively jester –
embarrassing, with outrageous gesture,
stiff respectability;
tumbling over dignity
in multi-coloured guides,
impudently prodding
deadly faces
into joy and laughter.
He only destroys
our pomp and vanity.

The Spirit is a lively bee –
buzzing elusively
through our solemnities.
He's not pinned down by resolutions,
but flies in dizzy revolutions
round our cultivated plots.
Sweet gifts he brings
of his own making;
and when he stings,
his heart is breaking.

Peter Dainty

Pentecost

(Whit Sunday)

Year C

Acts 2:1-21
  or Genesis 11:1-9
Psalm 104:26-34, 35b
Romans 8:14-17
  or Acts 2:1-21
John 14:8-17 (25-27)

All of them were filled with the Holy Spirit. (Acts 2:4a)

Prayer

O God may the fire of your Holy Spirit
consume in us all that displeases you,
and kindle in our hearts a burning zeal
for the service of your kingdom;
through Jesus Christ our Lord.

Adapted from an ancient collect

Hymn

The Spirit came at Pentecost
in unexpected ways
and loosed believing hearts and tongues
in floods of prayer and praise.

Discernment, healing, prophecy –
so many gifts he brought,
but all to make the Church mature
in deed and word and thought.

He showed them love and joy and peace
to kindle their desire
for lives producing godly fruit
and purified by fire.

With grace and tenderness he came,
as gently as a dove,
and whispered, 'Children, you belong
within your Father's love.'

A faithful witness to the truth,
as Advocate he came;
he stirred the saints to rise and go,
the Gospel to proclaim.

To blow the breath of life upon
the dying and the lost,
to bring them to a second birth,
he came at Pentecost.

We need your Holy Spirit, Lord,
today as much as then –
so send him to us now, we pray,
to fill our hearts again!

Martin E. Leckebusch

Metre: 8 6 8 6 (CM)
Suggested tune: *St Fulbert*

ORDINARY TIME

Trinity Sunday

Year A

Isaiah 40:12-17, 27-31
Psalm 8
2 Corinthians 13:11-13
Matthew 28:16-20

He gives power to the faint, and strengthens the powerless. (Isaiah 40:29)

Prayer

Blessed be God, Father, Son and Holy Spirit,
the Three in One,
the holy and wonderful Trinity
bound together in one eternity of love.
Blessed be God the Creator of all things.
Blessed be the Christ, our Saviour and Friend.
Blessed be the Spirit within us, our Guide and Strength.
Blessed be God for all that he is and all he has done.
Blessed be the One and the Three.

Holy God, we ask your blessing
upon all who are baptised and confirmed in the faith,
that they may witness to your presence and love.
We pray for preachers and teachers,
that they may seek to reveal
the mystery of your being with us.
Lord, guide the mission and outreach of your people.

Holy God, Holy and Strong One,
hear us and help us.
Amen.

David Adam

Poem

God of life, God of truth,
I rejoice that you are with me,
never distant or aloof.
Like a father, you are there,
reaching out your arms to hold me,
speaking words that show you care.

God of life, God of grace,
you have walked this earth before me,
giving truth a human face.
Knowing sorrow, knowing pain,
you were beaten, bruised and broken,
but in triumph rose again.

God of life, God of love –
felt as wind and tongues of fire
yet as gentle as a dove –
every moment, every hour,
you are working deep within me
through your sovereign selfless power.

God of life, God on high,
I can barely grasp your goodness,
language fails me when I try.
As a Father, through your Son,
by the Spirit you are with us,
somehow three, yet also one.

Nick Fawcett

Trinity Sunday

Year B

Isaiah 6:1-8
Psalm 29
Romans 8:12-17
John 3:1-17

For all who are led by the Spirit of God are children of God. (Romans 8:14)

Hymn

Children of God himself –
children he calls his own!
Ours is a way of peace
previously unknown:
the Spirit's leading makes us free
for all that we were meant to be.

'Abba, our Father God!'
Cry from our heart of hearts;
pledges that we are his
tenderly he imparts,
so we are merely echoing
the truth the Spirit comes to bring.

Each of us now his child,
each of us made an heir:
chosen with Christ our Lord,
all that is his to share,
for those who share his sufferings
will reign with him, the King of kings.

Martin E. Leckebusch

Metre: 6 6 6 6 88
Suggested tune: *Little Cornard*

Poem

May the grace of Christ uphold us.
May the Father's love enfold us.
May the Holy Spirit guide us,
so that with the Lord beside us,
we may go our way in peace. Amen.

Peter Dainty

Trinity Sunday
Year C

Proverbs 8:1-4, 22-31
Psalm 8
Romans 5:1-5
John 16:12-15

O Lord, our Sovereign, how majestic is your name in all the earth!
(Psalm 8:1)

Prayer

Blessed are you, Father, Son and Holy Spirit,
Three Persons in One God.
To you be praise and glory for ever.
In your goodness you have revealed yourself to us
and invited us to share in your glory.
Blessed are you, God, for ever.

Father, we give you thanks for your creation,
for the beauty and wonder of our world.
We ask your blessing upon all who work in caring
for the earth
and who labour to provide us with our daily needs.
May your Church lead others
to respect the world and each other.
We ask your blessing upon family life
and upon all relationships.

Holy, holy, holy God,
hear us and help us.
Amen.

David Adam

Hymn

Long ago the Father's voice
brought the universe to birth –
by his mighty Living Word
he created heaven and earth;
then he gave the gift of life
by the holy Breath he blew!
God eternal, One, yet Three,
all creation's source is you.

From before the dawn of time
chosen as the Father's own,
we receive this gift of grace
by the death of Christ alone;
now we feel the Spirit's touch –
power to set our lives ablaze!
God eternal, One, yet Three,
how we love your gracious ways!

God our Father makes his home
in each heart which loves the Son;
when we live as Jesus taught,
then the Father's will is done.
We shall know our Lord's commands
as we heed his Spirit's voice –
God eternal, One, yet Three,
glad obedience is our choice.

In the temple of the Lord,
Jesus is the cornerstone;
in our lives, both fruit and gifts
make his Spirit's presence known;
so the Church of God is built
to become a holy place:
God eternal, One, yet Three,
let your people grow in grace.

Father, we revere your name –
great Creator, sovereign King;
Jesus, Saviour, Son of God,
praise to you we gladly bring;
Holy Spirit, Breath of life,
you we honour and adore;
God eternal, One, yet Three,
be exalted evermore!

Martin E. Leckebusch

Metre: 7 7 7 7 D
Suggested tunes: *St Edmund; St George's Windsor*

Proper 4

Year A

Genesis 6:9-22; 7:24; 8:14-19
  or Deuteronomy 11:18-21, 26-28
Psalm 46
  or Psalm 31:1-5, 19-24
Romans 1:16, 17, 3:22b-28 (29-31)
Matthew 7:21-29

The house did not fall because it had been founded on rock. (Matthew 7:25b)

Prayer

Living God,
help us today, as we hear your word, to act upon it,
consecrating our lives to you
and committing ourselves again to your service.
Awaken us to all you would say,
and teach us to build our lives upon Christ,
our faith founded in him
so that it is able to withstand
whatever storms life may throw at it.
Speak now,
and give us ears to hear,
in his name.
Amen.

Nick Fawcett

Psalm 46

God is our refuge, God is our strength –
in our distress his presence is near;
so though the earth quake under our feet,
safe is his keeping, what shall we fear?

Constantly with us, faithful and strong –
God is our shield, our hope and our song.
Be still and know that he is the Lord,
ever revered and ever adored!

There is a city founded by God,
filled with his glory, held in his care;
nations may fall and kingdoms collapse –
still it remains that city we share:

Come, see his works, his marvellous deeds,
bringing to nought the power of the sword.
He is exalted over the earth –
humbly confess that he is the Lord:

Martin E. Leckebusch

Metre: 99 99 and refrain
Suggested tune: *Blessed Assurance*

Proper 4

Year B

1 Samuel 3:1-10 (11-20)
or Deuteronomy 5:12-15
Psalm 139:1-5, 12-18
or Psalm 81:1-10
2 Corinthians 4:5-12
Mark 2:23 – 3:6

He said to the man, 'Stretch out your hand'. (Mark 3:5)

Prayer

Blessed are you, Lord our God,
for you have created light to dispel the darkness
and have shone in our hearts
to give the light of the knowledge of the glory of God
in the face of Jesus Christ.
We rejoice that all power and might come from you.
Blessed be God for ever.

Loving God,
we pray for all who do not know or love you.
We remember especially
those who have hardened their hearts against you.
We pray for all whose life is joyless
or governed by rules rather than love.
May your Church be willing to accept and welcome
all who come seeking you and your love.
Teach us to be generous in our dealings with each other.

Lord, bringing light out of darkness,
let us share in your love.
Amen.

David Adam

Poem

And on the seventh day,
the day he rested
and looked at all he'd made
and called it good,
did God rejoice in snowflakes falling softly,
did he watch a wave's edge curl across the sand,
did he see the power of the oak within an acorn,
did he touch the fine green mosses with his hand?

Of course he did,
he who had dreamed and fashioned
all of the intricacy of our earth.
He loved, he loves and he will love for ever
every least particle to which his Word gave birth.

Elizabeth Rooney

Proper 4
Year C

1 Kings 18:20, 21 (22-29) 30-39
or 1 Kings 8:22, 23, 41-43
Psalm 96
or Psalm 96:1-9
Galatians 1:1-12
Luke 7:1-10

The Lord indeed is God; the Lord indeed is God. (1 Kings 18:39)

Prayer

Lord Jesus Christ,
inspire us and increase our faith as we worship you
through everything you have accomplished in so
many lives,
responding to people's cry for help
and ministering to their needs.
Inspire us through the faith of others:
their trust in your power and purpose,
their willingness to follow where you lead,
their confidence in your unfailing love.
Inspire us through the way the good news
continues to change lives,
capturing the hearts of individuals the world over,
their faith often putting *ours* to shame.
Speak to us now,
so that we might trust you more,
love you better
and serve you more effectively,
to the glory of your name.
Amen.

Nick Fawcett

Psalm 96

Bring to God your new, best songs,
all creation;
raise a hymn of gratitude
for salvation;
far and wide, throughout the world,
sound his glory;
he has done amazing things –
tell the story.

Earth and heavens, revere the Lord,
your creator;
why exalt some other god?
He is greater!
His are strength and majesty
never-ending;
ours, the privilege of praise,
voices blending.

With the finest you possess
bow before him;
from the fullness of your heart,
come, adore him.
See, his beauty floods the earth –
holy splendour!
Yield to him in reverent fear –
glad surrender!

All that lurks in human hearts
he discloses;
all that fails the test of truth,
he opposes.
Let the earth rejoice in hope
of his kingdom;
skies and oceans, trees and fields,
join the anthem!

Martin E. Leckebusch

Metre: 74 74 D
Suggested tune: *Gwalchmai*

Proper 5
Year A

Genesis 12:1-9
or Hosea 5:15 – 6:6
Psalm 33:1-12
or Psalm 50:7-15
Romans 4:13-25
Matthew 9:9-13, 18-26

Take heart, daughter; your faith has made you well. (Matthew 9:22)

Prayer

Living God,
we come to you,
not because we have any claim on your goodness,
or any right to expect your blessing,
but because, in your love, you invite us here,
delighting in our worship and glad to call us your children.
Yet we come too knowing that worship without response is empty,
and words without deeds are hollow.
So we ask, by your grace,
that you will deepen our knowledge of you
and help us to love you as much as you love us,
through Jesus Christ our Lord.
Amen.

Nick Fawcett

Hymn

Show me how to stand for justice:
how to work for what is right,
how to challenge false assumptions,
how to walk within the light.
May I learn to share more freely
in a world so full of greed,
showing your immense compassion
by the life I choose to lead.

Teach my heart to treasure mercy,
whether given or received –
for my need has not diminished
since the day I first believed:
let me seek no satisfaction
boasting of what I have done,
but rejoice that I am pardoned
and accepted in your Son.

Gladly I embrace a lifestyle
modelled on your living word,
in humility submitting
to the truth which I have heard.
Make me conscious of your presence
every day, in all I do:
by your Spirit's gracious prompting
May I learn to walk with you.

Martin E. Leckebusch

Metre: 8 7 8 7 D
Suggested tunes: *Abbot's Leigh; Hyfrydol*

Proper 5

Year B

1 Samuel 8:4-11 (12-15)
16-20 (11:14, 15)
or Genesis 3:8-15
Psalm 138
or Psalm 130
2 Corinthians 4:13 – 5:1
Mark 3:20-35

I wait for the Lord, my soul waits, and in his word I hope. (Psalm 130:5)

Prayer

Father in heaven,
you speak to us in many ways.
Even when you are silent, you still speak to us,
in order to examine us,
to try us,
and so that the hour of understanding
may be more profound.
Oh, in the time of silence,
when I remain alone and abandoned
because I do not hear your voice,
it seems as if the separation must last for ever,
but, Father, it is only a moment of silence in the intimacy of a conversation.
Bless, then, this silence
and let me not forget that you are silent through love,
and that you speak through love,
so that in your silence and in your word
you are still the same Father,
and that you guide and instruct even by your silence.
Amen.

Nick Fawcett

Poem

I'm here, Lord.
Can you hear me?
I'm lost, Lord,
in an alien world,
like a drop-out from heaven.
I've fallen from the light
into the darkness
and the clouds of glory have long gone.
I'm phoning home because
I need to hear a friendly voice,
some reassurance, comfort, hope,
some guidance and advice – anything.
I need to know you're still there,
and that you know I'm here,
lonely and afraid.
Answer me, Lord.
I'm holding the receiver to my ear.
Can you hear the tone?
It's urgent, Lord.
I'm waiting, Lord.
Can't you hear it ringing,
ringing, ringing, ringing, ringing . . . ?

Peter Dainty

Proper 5

Year C

1 Kings 17:8-16 (17-24)
or 1 Kings 17:17-24
Psalm 146
or Psalm 30
Galatians 1:11-24
Luke 7:11-17

See, your son is alive. (1 Kings 17:23b)

Prayer

Blessed are you, Father, Son and Holy Spirit.
You have created light and life
and you offer to us your light and your life.
In you we triumph over death
and are given the gift of eternal life.
Blessed are you, one God for ever and ever.

We give thanks to you, O Father,
that in Jesus is the resurrection and the life,
and that through him we have the victory over death.
We give thanks for the Good News of the Gospel
and pray for all who seek to proclaim your love and salvation.
We ask your blessing on all who preach the word and who administer the sacraments.
We pray especially for those who are working
with the under-privileged and marginalised of the world.

Strong and saving God,
hear us and help us.
Amen.

David Adam

Poem

Holy Weaver, may we watch you
guiding life's complexity?
From the threads of joy and sadness,
deftly twining pain and gladness,
you create a single hanging –
one eternal tapestry.

We will listen, truthful Poet –
listen to your words of grace:
human cries of faith and passion,
grief and hope, you take and fashion
in the saga, yet unfolding,
of your dealings with our race.

Skilful Artist, how we trust you,
place our hope in you alone:
on a canvas stained with sorrow
you can paint a bright tomorrow
and, with unimagined colours,
make your sovereign purpose known.

We adore you, mighty Goldsmith:
all to you we gladly yield!
Jeweller in eternal treasure,
for your good and holy pleasure
take our lives, refine and shape us
till your glory is revealed.

Martin E. Leckebusch

Proper 6

Year A

Genesis 18:1-15 (21:1-7)
  or Exodus 19:2-8a
Psalm 116:1, 10-17
  or Psalm 100
Romans 5:1-8
Matthew 9:35 – 10:8 (9-23)

The harvest is plentiful, but the labourers are few. (Matthew 9:37)

Prayer

Blessed are you, Lord our God,
for you have called us into life and to love you.
You have called us to proclaim your love and power
in all the world.
Lord, send us out in the power of your Spirit,
that we may tell of you and your abiding presence.
Blessed are you, Father, Son and Holy Spirit.

Lord, we ask your blessing upon your Church,
that we may show signs of being One in you,
holy and dedicated to being apostolic
as we reach out to all peoples.
We pray for all who are reaching out to others
in your name and in love.
Bless and guide all who preach the word
and all who share in your healing ministry.
We remember those who work to relieve the
  distress and sorrow
of people and nations.

Lord, as you have called us,
hear us and help us.
Amen.

David Adam

Poem

Lord, make me an instrument of your peace:
where there is hatred, let me sow love,
where there is injury, pardon,
where there is doubt, faith,
where there is darkness, light,
where there is despair, hope,
and where there is sadness, joy.

Divine Master,
grant that I may not so much seek to be consoled
  as to console,
to be understood as to understand,
to be loved as to love.
For it is in giving that we receive,
it is in pardoning that we are pardoned,
and in dying that we are born to eternal life.
Amen.

St Francis of Assisi

Proper 6

Year B

1 Samuel 15:34 – 16:13
or Ezekiel 17:22-24
Psalm 20
or Psalm 92:1-4, 12-15
2 Corinthians 5:6-10 (11-13) 14-17
Mark 4:26-34

All the trees of the field shall know that I am the Lord. (Ezekiel 17:24)

Prayer

Loving God,
by your grace plant new seeds of faith within us today,
and through your Spirit feed and nurture them,
so that, however small that faith might be,
it might grow and flourish within us
beyond anything we might imagine.
Grow in our lives,
that we might sow seeds in the lives of others,
each of us, through our life and witness,
insignificant in themselves,
contributing to the expansion of your kingdom,
the furthering of your will on earth,
as it is in heaven.
Amen.

Nick Fawcett

Hymn

Lord Jesus, plant a seed of faith
and let it grow in me,
to bear a harvest shown by deeds
of lasting quality.

Grant me a gentle, humble heart
where love alone holds sway,
till selfless servanthood becomes
my habit day by day.

Give me a deeper, richer hope,
a vision sure and clear,
to strengthen me until the day
when you at last appear.

I have no faith but what you give;
your love has made me new;
my hope is found in no one else –
Lord, give me more of you!

Martin E. Leckebusch

Metre: 8 6 8 6 (CM)
Suggested tunes: *Abridge; Martyrdom*

Proper 6

Year C

1 Kings 21:1-10 (11-14) 15-21a
 or 2 Samuel 11:26 – 12:10, 13-15
Psalm 5:1-8
 or Psalm 32
Galatians 2:15-21
Luke 7:36 – 8:3

Your sins are forgiven. (Luke 7:48)

Prayer

Blessed are you, Father, Son and Holy Spirit,
for you welcome us into your presence.
You forgive our sins and give us the power,
through contact with you,
to walk in newness of life.
In your love you accept us and offer us eternal life.
Blessed are you for ever.

We give thanks for all who have come to know
the joy of your forgiveness
through the ministry of your Church.
Help us to know that,
though you do not love the sin,
you do love and accept the sinner.
We pray for all who share in healing and
 forgiveness.
We ask you to bless all who care for others,
all who preach the word,
those who administer the sacraments
and those who counsel any who are in trouble.

Lord, we come to you:
hear us and help us.
Amen.

David Adam

Poem

My sin, however great,
still cannot be
greater than God's forgiveness.
There will,
I think there almost must be,
pain –
the pain of knowing
how I've wounded Love.
And there must be
a turning back to him.
Facing what I have done,
what I've become,
and seeing as he sees.

But, oh, then comes
the sinking to my knees
in joy and praise
that Love can love me still,
can love and always has,
and always will.

Elizabeth Rooney

Proper 7

Year A

Genesis 21:8-21
  or Jeremiah 20:7-13
Psalm 86:1-10, 16-17
  or Psalm 69:8-11 (12-17) 18-20
Romans 6:1b-11
Matthew 10:24-39

But the Lord is with me like a dread warrior. (Jeremiah 20:11a)

Prayer

Blessed are you, Lord our God,
for you created this world out of your goodness
and pour your love upon it.
All things are precious in your sight
and all are valued.
Blessed are you, Father, Son and Holy Spirit.

God, our Protection and Strength,
we bring before you
all who are suffering for their faith,
all who are mocked, scorned, rejected
and in danger.
We remember those imprisoned
and those who suffer physical harm.
We pray for all who seek to proclaim your love
and to help in the healing of nations.
We ask your blessing
upon the Church to which we belong
and pray that we may use aright
the resources you have given us.

God, in your love and mercy,
hear us and help us.
Amen.

David Adam

Poem

I do not know what life may hold,
if good or ill I'll see,
what twists and turns may yet unfold,
what trials yet might be.
I cannot say if light will shine
or darkness fall once more,
what destiny might still be mine,
what future lies in store.
But even if the way is tough
and storms begin to blow,
the gales prove strong, the water rough,
one thing, Lord, still I know:
that you'll be there, supporting me,
a faithful, loving guide –
a constant help who will not fail
to strengthen and provide.
I have no need to ask for more
nor any cause to fear:
whatever life may hold for me
I know that you'll be near.

Nick Fawcett

Proper 7

Year B

1 Samuel 17 (1a, 4-11, 19-23) 32-49
 or Job 38:1-11
Psalm 9:9-20
 or 1 Samuel 17:57 – 18:5, 10-16
 or Psalm 133
 or Psalm 107:1-3, 23-32
2 Corinthians 6:1-13
Mark 4:35-41

The battle is the Lord's. (1 Samuel 17:47)

Prayer

Blessed are you, Lord our God,
for you are ever with us
and your presence brings us close
to your power and your peace.
You are ready to hear our cry
and to help us in our troubles.
We rejoice in your love and in your care.
Blessed are you, God, for ever, Father, Son and
 Holy Spirit.

Almighty and loving God,
we seek to rest in your presence and in your peace.
The Church is often buffeted
by storms of antagonism and opposition.
We remember before you all Christians
who are struggling to survive in areas
where they face violence or ridicule for their faith.
We pray especially for those
whose lives are at risk at this time.
We remember also young Christians
who have to face opposition from their friends
 and relatives.

Lord, in the storms of life we call upon you:
grant us your peace.
Amen.

David Adam

Poem

Whether I fly with angels, fall with dust,
 Thy hands made both, and I am there:
Thy power and love, my love and trust
 Make one place everywhere.

George Herbert

Proper 7

Year C

1 Kings 19:1-4 (5-7) 8-15a
  or Isaiah 65:1-9
Psalms 42, 43
  or Psalm 22:19-28
Galatians 3:23-29
Luke 8:26-39

He came and sat down under a solitary broom tree. (1 Kings 19:4)

Prayer

Blessed are you, Lord our God,
for you created order out of chaos
and the world out of your love.
You offer peace and well-being
to all of your creation.
Blessed are you, Father, Son and Holy Spirit.

We give thanks to you, O Lord,
for all who help to bring healing and peace to
  your world.
May the Church be seen as an instrument
of your peace and of your love for all peoples.
May all who are distressed and disturbed
come to know the peace of Christ and his love.
We ask your blessing upon all meditation groups
and all who help others to live in harmony.

Christ, our Lord,
grant us your peace.
Amen.

David Adam

Poem

Are you listening? Are you here?
Come and save me. Lord, draw near.
Day by day I'm losing hope,
fearful that I may not cope.
Trust is weak and faith is frail,
stretched until it starts to fail.
Yet I've felt this way before
and, despite it, you proved sure,
bringing joy instead of tears,
inner peace in place of fears.
Though I'm weak, Lord, you are strong,
there to help my whole life long.

Nick Fawcett

Proper 8

Year A

Genesis 22:1-14
  or Jeremiah 28:5-9
Psalm 13
  or Psalm 89:1-4, 15-18
Romans 6:12-23
Matthew 10:40-42

Happy are the people . . . who walk, O Lord, in the light of your countenance.
(Psalm 89:15)

Prayer

Gracious God,
we dare to draw near,
not through any merit of our own
but trusting in your great mercy –
redeemed, renewed and restored
through the love of Christ.
Set us free from all that holds us captive;
we gladly surrender our lives to your service,
to be used as you will.
As you have given,
so we give back,
in the name of Christ.
Amen.

Nick Fawcett

Poem (Psalm 13)

When anxious thoughts assail my mind,
when I begin to doubt your care,
when gloom and sorrow flood my soul,
I bring my fears to you, my God, in prayer.

I call to you to answer soon,
to turn my darkness into light,
for life can be a battlefield –
unless you help me, I shall lose the fight!

Yet in your endless love I trust,
in your salvation I rejoice:
because you have been good to me
I offer you my praise with heart and voice.

Martin E. Leckebusch

Proper 8

Year B

2 Samuel 1:1, 17-27
  or Wisdom of Solomon
    1:13-15; 2:23,24
Psalm 130
  or *Canticle:* Lamentations 3:23-33
  or Psalm 30
2 Corinthians 8:7-15
Mark 5:21-43

Weeping may linger for the night, but joy comes with the morning. (Psalm 30:5b)

Prayer

Sovereign God,
give us a sense of your nearness as we worship you,
so that we might hear your voice
and learn more of your love in Christ.
Teach us through his life and ministry,
and through all those who, across the years,
have experienced his power
and felt the touch of his hand in their lives,
to respond in turn,
bringing our broken lives and broken world to him,
and opening all to his healing, restoring and life-giving love.
Amen.

Nick Fawcett

Psalm

I will sing your mercies, Lord,
how you heard and answered prayer:
foes disarmed and fears relieved –
you have lifted my despair.

Your displeasure swiftly fades,
even when your anger burns;
though the night is full of tears,
with the dawn our joy returns.

I have tasted both extremes,
confidence and deep dismay:
from your strength, security;
from your silence, disarray.

In profound distress I prayed:
'Gracious God, prolong my days –
can the grave extol your name?
Let me live, and sing your praise!'

Then my grief was turned to joy;
then my laughter was restored –
one unending song of thanks
I will bring to you, my Lord.

Martin E. Leckebusch

Metre: 77 77

Suggested tunes: *Newington; University College*

Proper 8

Year C

2 Kings 2:1-2, 6-14
or 1 Kings 19:5-16, 19-21
Psalm 77:1, 2, 11-20
or Psalm 16
Galatians 5:1, 13-25
Luke 9:51-62

Let me kiss my father and my mother, and then I will follow you.
(1 Kings 19:20)

Prayer

Lord Jesus Christ,
teach us today to put you first in our lives,
seeking to honour and serve you not as an afterthought,
an optional extra,
or as an occasional pursuit,
but wholeheartedly,
genuinely committed to you with body, mind and spirit.
May our response to you shape everything we do,
rather than everything we do put time for you on hold.
Call us afresh now
and help us truly to be your people,
by your grace.
Amen.

Nick Fawcett

Poem

A fox has a hole
and a bird has a nest
but Jesus has nowhere
to lay down and rest.
He travels the earth
like a clown or a tramp,
and he knows what it's like
in a refugee camp.

Jesus, wanderer,
travelling alone;
knocking on doors
in search of a home.

He's one with the outcast
who's branded at birth.
He's one with the stranger
and pilgrim on earth.
He's one with the poor man
of no fixed address.
He sits with the lonely
and shares their distress.

Jesus, wanderer,
travelling alone;
knocking on doors
in search of a home.

Peter Dainty

Proper 9

Year A

Genesis 24:34-38, 42-49, 58-67
or Zechariah 9:9-12
Psalm 45:10-17
or *Canticle:* Song of Solomon 2:8-13
or Psalm 145:8-15
Romans 7:15-25a
Matthew 11:16-19, 25-30

Arise, my love, my fair one, and come away. (Song of Songs 2:10)

Prayer

Speak, Lord, for your servant hears.
Grant us ears to hear,
Eyes to see,
Wills to obey,
Hearts to love;
Then declare what you will,
Reveal what you will,
Command what you will,
Demand what you will.

Christina Rossetti

Poem

He gives us burdens of delight
and fits our yokes exactly right.
His burden's light,
his burden's light.

He is a god of love and fire
who knows our deepest heart's desire.
He burdens us with joy, with grace
and fits them gently into place.
His longing love would see us blest.
We find his burdens fit us best.

Elizabeth Rooney

Proper 9

Year B

2 Samuel 5:1-5, 9, 10
or Ezekiel 2:1-5
Psalm 48
or Psalm 123
2 Corinthians 12:2-10
Mark 6:1-13

Great is the Lord and greatly to be praised in the city of our God. (Psalm 48:1)

Prayer

Blessed are you, Lord God, giver of life and light.
You give us of your love: you give us of yourself.
Open our ears to your call and our hearts to
your love.
Send us out in the power of your Spirit
to proclaim the Good News of your saving love
as revealed in our Saviour Jesus Christ.
Blessed are you, Father, Son and Holy Spirit.

We give thanks that you sent Jesus to live among us.
We pray that we may share in his mission,
that we may pass on the message of the Gospel
and show acts of mercy that reveal God's love.
May your whole Church be moved to share
in the ministry that is theirs.
We remember today all involved in the healing
ministry.
We ask you to bless all counsellors, spiritual
directors
and all who lead us in our ministry.

Lord, hear us:
show us your loving kindness.
Amen.

David Adam

Poem (Psalm 48)

The Lord who reigns in Zion
has made his glory known:
how splendid is the city
he chose to be his own,
for there he has established
his presence and his throne.

When Zion faced an onslaught
of fierce hostility,
her enemies were routed
and swiftly forced to flee –
the God who lives within her
is her security.

There, in God's holy temple,
his love compels our gaze;
his righteousness inspires us
to fill the world with praise,
until our friends and neighbours
are drawn to seek his ways.

And every generation
can learn from those before,
yet find in Zion's beauty
new riches to explore;
our God is with his people,
both now and evermore!

Martin E. Leckebusch

Proper 9
Year C

2 Kings 5:1-14
or Isaiah 66:10-14
Psalm 30
or Psalm 66:1-8
Galatians 6:(1-6) 7-16
Luke 10:1-11, 16-20

Ask the Lord of the harvest to send out labourers into his harvest. (Luke 10:2)

Prayer

Blessed are you, Lord our God,
for you reach out to each of us
in love and in peace.
You offer us your healing and power
and you call us to share in telling this Good News
to all people.
Blessed are you, Father, Son and Holy Spirit.

We give thanks to you, O Lord,
for the good news of the Gospel.
We ask your blessing upon all who seek
to share in the mission and outreach of Christ.
May the Church grow in holiness,
in outreach and in number.
We pray for missionary societies
and for all who are seeking to spread the good news.
Grant that we may share in this mission.

Lord of the harvest,
may your kingdom come in us.
Amen.

David Adam

Poem

Take the life I proffer,
loving God, today;
all the gifts I offer,
all I think and say.
What I am and what I do,
these I give you now.
Lord, I want to serve you –
show me where and how.

Nick Fawcett

Proper 10

Year A

Genesis 25:19-34
or Isaiah 55:10-13
Psalm 119:105-112
or Psalm 65:(1-7) 8-13
Romans 8:1-11
Matthew 13:1-9, 18-23

Let anyone with ears listen! (Matthew 13:9)

Prayer

Blessed are you, Lord our God,
for you come to us
and seek to make your home with us.
Let our doors and our ears be open to you.
Let our hearts find their rest and their joy in you,
that we may grow in grace and live to your glory.
Blessed are you, Father, Son and Holy Spirit.

Loving God,
hear us and help us.
Amen.

David Adam

Poem

A preacher went forth to preach,
and, as he preached,
some words fell by the wayside
into the ears of causal visitors
to holy places on special occasions;
and these unprepared strangers
could not understand the alien language
of an exclusive religion;
and they remained unimpressed
even by the crushing handshakes
and the hard seats.

And some of the preacher's words fell
among the sedimentary rocks
of conventional worship –
like polished pebbles, echoing and clattering,
and adding another layer to a dead tradition.

And some words floated like thistledown
among the prolific weeds
of humdrum thinking;
they settled, without taking root,
among the choking tendrils
of mediocre expectations.

And some words fell onto the good ground
of minds and hearts
open, eager and hungry;
but the words themselves
were like dry pellets
that even the birds would spit out –
pieces of grit, which sometimes sparkle,
but have no power,
except to blind searching eyes.

And the preacher returned
to his lonely chamber
without even a twofold harvest.
'What use to curse the soil
if the seed is sterile?'
God told him.
'Come close to me in life and prayer
and listen for my Word;
look again into the treasury of Scripture
and I will show you seed
potent enough to bear fruit
in all weathers;
and a lamp bright enough
to guide the feet of pilgrims
through the valley of shadows;
and a sword, sharp enough
to pierce to the very heart.'

Peter Dainty

Proper 10

Year B

2 Samuel 6:1-5, 12b-19
or Amos 7:7-15
Psalm 24
or Psalm 85:8-13
Ephesians 1:3-14
Mark 6:14-29

David danced before the Lord with all his might. (2 Samuel 6:14a)

Prayer

Blessed are you, the God and Father of our Lord Jesus Christ,
who has blessed us with every spiritual blessing.
You have destined us for the glorious freedom
of the children of God.
You have given us of your love and of yourself.
May we rejoice in your rule
and in the coming of your kingdom.
Blessed are you, Father, Son and Holy Spirit,
one God for ever and ever.

David Adam

Psalm 24

Let every door be opened wide:
The Lord return, his battles done –
he takes his throne, the glorious King,
by whom the fiercest fight was won.

His realm extends to all he made:
the earth; the riches it contains;
the heights and depths of human life –
throughout the universe he reigns.

But in his presence who can stand?
Who dares to seek his holy face?
How can our hearts and hands be pure
but by his favour and his grace?

Let every heart be opened wide:
our Lord returns, his battles done –
he takes his throne, our glorious King,
whose gracious reign has now begun.

Martin E. Leckebusch

Metre: 88 88 (LM)
Suggested tunes: *Gonfalon Royal; Truro*

Proper 10

Year C

Amos 7:7-17
  or Deuteronomy 30:9-14
Psalm 82
  or Psalm 25:1-10
Colossians 1:1-14
Luke 10:25-37

But a Samaritan while travelling came near him; and when he saw him, he was moved with pity. (Luke 10:33)

Prayer

Blessed are you, Lord our God.
You come to us in our need.
You bind up our wounds and restore us to life.
May we be good neighbours
to all who are in need or distress
and so share in your saving love.
Blessed are you, Father, Son and Holy Spirit.

Lord God,
as you have called us to work with you,
show us the ways of your salvation.
May your Church care for the weak and defenceless,
for the needy and the poor.
Let us never avoid our responsibility
and pass by on the other side.
We pray for the work of the Samaritans
and for all relief organisations.

Show us your ways, O Lord,
and teach us your paths.
Amen.

David Adam

Hymn

Open our eyes to see
the anguish of the poor –
indignities untold
where life is insecure;
then may our ears discern your call
to demonstrate your care for all.

Open our minds to grasp
life's grim reality –
how greed and power prolong
the curse of poverty;
and fill our mouths with words to speak,
defending those whose voice is weak.

Open our hands to give,
to serve through all our deeds,
and let our strength be spent
to meet our neighbours' needs;
let love, not duty, be our guide:
Lord, let our hearts be open wide!

Martin E. Leckebusch

Metre: 6 6 6 6 88
Suggested tune: *Love Unknown*

Proper 11

Year A

Genesis 28:10-19a
  or Wisdom of Solomon 12:13, 16-19
  or Isaiah 44:6-8
Psalm 139:1-11, 23, 24
  or Psalm 86:11-17
Romans 8:12-25
Matthew 13:24-30, 36-43

Know that I am with you and will keep you wherever you go.
(Genesis 28:15)

Prayer

God of justice and truth,
yet also of love and mercy,
focus our thoughts on you,
so that we are open to fresh insights into truth,
new horizons in faith
and a deeper understanding of your purpose.
Help us to stand up against evil
and to work together for good,
recognising that you yearn to redeem all
and do not willingly let go of anyone.
So may we contribute to your kingdom's growth
  among us now,
through Jesus Christ our Lord,
Amen.

Nick Fawcett

Poem

Twice God spoke to Jacob
in the desert night –
once as he slept and dreamed,
once as he fought till morning light.

Jacob the deceiver
fled to a desert land
he made a rock his pillow,
his bed was the stony sand.

But God is always with us,
wherever we may go;
and heaven is nearer than we think
here in this world below.

He dreamed an angel ladder
stretching to the sky
and saw that heaven was only
a flight of stairs away.

He woke in fear and trembling,
completely overawed,
and made his rocky pillow
an altar to the Lord.

For God is always with us,
wherever we may go;
and heaven is nearer than we think
here in this world below.

He felt that he was standing
at heaven's very door
and vowed to serve the Lord his God
here on heav'n's ground floor.

Later, Jacob wrestled
throughout the long dark night,
but though it left him wounded
God blest him in the fight.

For God is always with us,
wherever we may go;
and heaven is nearer than we think
here in this world below.

Peter Dainty

Proper 11

Year B

2 Samuel 7:1-14a
 or Jeremiah 23:1-6
Psalm 89:20-37
 or Psalm 23
Ephesians 2:11-22
Mark 6:30-34, 53-56

He makes me lie down in green pastures. (Psalm 23:2a)

Prayer

Living God,
you know our needs better than we know them
 ourselves,
you alone seeing into the heart
and being able to offer real peace,
enduring happiness
and true fulfilment.
So we come,
not to besiege you with requests
or plague you with demands,
but asking simply that you will work within us
as you deem best,
drawing us closer to you and increasing our faith.
Help us to focus above all on your kingdom
 and your righteousness,
in the knowledge that you delight to give all we need
and so much more,
through Jesus Christ our Lord.
Amen.

Nick Fawcett

Psalm 23

Within the busy rush of life
 I find a resting-place:
when I submit to Christ my Lord
 and let him set my pace
he shows the way that I should take
 whatever trails I face.

Amid the choices I must make
 and duties that increase
he comes to calm my anxious thoughts,
 to make the turmoil cease;
as in his presence I remain
 he guides me into peace.

The timeless, all-sufficient God
 my every longing knows
and daily he refreshes me
 with joy which overflows;
anointed by tranquillity
 my strength to serve him grows.

My Saviour bids me walk with him
 and follow all his ways –
his plan for me is fruitfulness
 throughout my earthly days,
since now and evermore I live
 beneath his loving gaze.

Martin E. Leckebusch

Metre: 86 86 86
Suggested tune: *Brother James' Air*

Proper 11

Year C

Amos 8:1-12
  or Genesis 18:1-10a
Psalm 52
  or Psalm 15
Colossians 1:15-28
Luke 10:38-42

There is need of only one thing. Mary has chosen the better part, which will not be taken away from her. (Luke 10:42)

Prayer

Sovereign God,
help us, as we gather here once more,
truly to focus on you;
to direct our thoughts away
from the pressures, demands and responsibilities
  of another week;
away from anxieties and difficulties,
trivial distractions and irrelevancies.
Help us to listen again to your word
and hear what you would say to us,
so that we might return to the daily routine,
whatever it might hold,
strengthened and encouraged,
with deeper insight and a fresh perspective,
through Jesus Christ our Lord.
Amen.

Nick Fawcett

Poem

Why don't you give up, God?
You know me by now –
the churning restlessness,
the worrying, and how
tense and distracted I am.

You keep asking me
to stop fussing and play,
to relax and rejoice
and admire your new day.
I'm busy, Lord.
I have things to do,
Like Martha, I am never through.

Yes, I know Mary chose
the better part,
simply stopped still
and opened up her heart.
It's something I would really
like to do
but not right now. Right now
I'm much too busy
for you.

Elizabeth Rooney

Proper 12

Year A

Genesis 29:15-28
or 1 Kings 3:5-12
Psalm 105:1-11, 45b
or Psalm 128
or Psalm 119:129-136
Romans 8:26-39
Matthew 13:31-33, 44-52

The kingdom of heaven is like treasure hidden in a field. (Matthew 13:44a)

Prayer

Blessed are you, Lord our God,
for you have given us of your kingdom.
You invite us to share in your godly rule
and in the riches of life that is eternal.
Lord, teach us to seek you
until we know you and love you
and are aware of your transforming power in all the world.
Blessed are you, Father, Son and Holy Spirit.

We ask your blessing upon all who seek
to proclaim the Good News of your kingdom.
We pray for preachers of the word
and ministers of the sacraments,
for evangelists and all who witness in their daily lives
to your presence and power.
We remember those who quietly transform their surroundings for the better
and those who show others of your kingdom in their midst.

Lord, your kingdom come,
in us as it is in heaven.
Amen.

David Adam

Poem

I've talked of trusting come what may,
of walking where you lead;
I've pledged to follow day by day,
to serve in word and deed;
I've claimed to love you, heart and soul,
enough to give my all –
yet though such faith has been my goal
repeatedly I fall.

Lord, thankfully the love you show
is of a different kind –
a love that will not let me go
no matter what you find.
However much I fail to be
the person I intend,
in you I find true constancy,
one faithful to the end.

Nick Fawcett

Proper 12

Year B

2 Samuel 11:1-15
    or 2 Kings 4:42-44
Psalm 14
    or Psalm 145:10-19
Ephesians 3:14-21
John 6:1-21

Gather up the fragments left over, so that nothing may be lost. (John 6:12)

Prayer

Blessed are you, Lord our God,
in your love and care for your creation.
You do not turn away any who come to you.
You come to meet the seekers
and provide refreshment
for all who hunger and thirst.
You care for the broken and the fragmented
and want nothing to be lost.
Blessed are you, Father, Son and Holy Spirit.

We come to you, dear Lord, as seekers;
we are hungry for your love and your care.
We ask you to bless all who are pilgrims and seekers,
all who long for an awareness of your presence
    and your power.
We remember before you
all who bring healing and refreshment to your people.
We pray for preachers and pastors,
for leaders of prayer groups and retreat conductors
and for all places of pilgrimage.

Lord, have mercy:
let us know your compassion and care.
Amen.

David Adam

Poem

When Jesus asked his friends
to feed the hungry crowd,
they said,
'It's far too late today;
we can't afford to pay;
let's send them all away
to feed themselves.'

But Jesus answered,
'No. You will not need a lot.
Find out how much you've got.'

They came again to him and said,
'We've only found two fish
and these five loaves of bread;
but what's the use of them
among so many?'

Jesus replied,
'It is enough. You need
no more than this to feed
these hungry people.'

However big your task,
if only you will ask,
you're sure to find enough –
enough to start with.

They gave him what they had
and he looked up to heaven,
giving thanks to God.
And then he told his friends
to share the food
among the people
sitting on the ground;
and that's when,
to their great surprise,
they found
there was enough
to go around.

However big your task,
if only you will ask,
God will provide enough
to go along with.

After the people had been fed,
the friends of Jesus
picked up all the pieces
of the fish and bread
that were left over,
so that nothing
should be wasted,
and they filled
twelve baskets
with the food
that people
had not even tasted.

However big your task,
if only you will ask,
God gives you more than enough,
to finish with.

Peter Dainty

Proper 12

Year C

Hosea 1:2-10
  or Genesis 18:20-32
Psalm 85
  or Psalm 138
Colossians 2:6-15 (16-19)
Luke 11:1-13

Knock, and the door will be opened for you. (Luke 11:9)

Prayer

Blessed are you, God and Father of us all.
You created us out of your love
and redeemed us by your love.
We rejoice that you sustain us with your love
and that you never leave us.
We seek to know your presence
and to give our love to you.
Blessed are you, God, for ever.

As we rejoice in your love for all people,
may your Church strive for justice and freedom
  for all.
We remember all who are persecuted for their faith
and all who are oppressed by tyranny.
We ask your blessing upon all who witness
to the power of prayer and knowing you.
We pray for religious communities
and for all who preach the word
and administer the sacraments.

Father, your kingdom come in us
as it is in heaven.
Amen.

David Adam

Poem

Father, teach me how to pray,
for I don't know what to say,
sometimes so unsure I barely say a word.
Grant me strength to persevere,
keeping faith that you are near
even though it often seems you haven't heard.
Help me share what's deep inside,
doubts and fears I try to hide,
faults and weaknesses I hesitate to name.
Give me faith to bare my soul,
trusting you can make me whole,
set me free from any sense of guilt and shame.
Help me share my hopes and fears,
joy and laughter, pain and tears,
knowing every part of life is your concern.
And to comprehend your will,
teach me also to be still,
so that through your Spirit's prompting I might
  learn.
Bid me come because I may,
not because I'm told to pray,
but responding to the welcome you extend –
neither nervous nor in dread
but approaching you instead
as a faithful father, living, loving friend.

Nick Fawcett

Proper 13

Year A

Genesis 32:22-31
or Isaiah 55:1-5
Psalm 17:1-7, 16
or Psalm 145:8, 9, 15-22
Romans 9:1-5
Matthew 14:13-21

He had compassion for them and cured their sick. (Matthew 14:14b)

Prayer

Sovereign God,
we bring you our spiritual hunger,
our yearning for inner contentment,
knowing that you alone can feed our souls,
and do so in ways exceeding all our expectations.
Come, then, now,
and reach out to all gathered here today,
filling us with spiritual food –
bread of life and living water –
so that we may go on our way,
nourished,
filled,
truly satisfied.
Amen.

Nick Fawcett

Poem

Why don't I trust you, Lord?
You've never sent me
anything but good.

I take your gifts
and listen for the tick,
then soak them
in cold, wet suspiciousness.
I'm sure the bread is stone,
the fish, as poisonous
as any scorpion's sting.

I never seem to remember
that the men
who ate the loaves and fishes
you had blessed
were nourished,
not made ill.

Why do I greet your tenderness,
your love for me,
with such ill will?

Elizabeth Rooney

Proper 13

Year B

2 Samuel 11:26 – 12:13a
  or Exodus 16:2-4, 9-15
Psalm 51:1-13
  or Psalm 78:23-29
Ephesians 4:1-16
John 6:24-35

This is the bread that the Lord has given you to eat. (Exodus 16:15b)

Prayer

Living God,
in a world that looks for instant satisfaction,
quick fixes,
fast food,
we turn again to you,
seeking eternal fulfilment,
lasting renewal
and enduring nourishment through Christ.
Meet with us, we pray,
and feed us once more,
in body, mind and spirit.
Amen.

Nick Fawcett

Hymn

For every word which feeds us
  by nourishing the soul,
which satisfies our hunger
  and makes our spirits whole;
for milk and meat, we thank you,
  for strength to face the fight;
for truth which we can savour,
  our comfort and delight;
for Scriptures which were written
  by those your Spirit stirred –
but most of all we thank you
  for Christ, the living Word!

For bread which speaks so clearly
  of all that you have done
and wine which tells the anguish
  by which our peace was won;
for all that spells forgiveness,
  a pardon for the past;
for hope which we can cherish,
  a promise which will last;
we thank you for the table
  where such a feast is spread –
but most of all we thank you
  for Christ, the living Bread!

Martin E. Leckebusch

Metre: 13 13 13 13 13 13
Suggested tune: *Thaxted*

Proper 13

Year C

Hosea 11:1-11
 or Ecclesiastes 1: 2, 12-14; 2:18-23
Psalm 107:1-9, 43
 or Psalm 49:1-12
Colossians 3:1-11
Luke 12:13-21

Take care! Be on your guard against all kinds of greed. (Luke 12:15)

Prayer

Loving God,
remind us again today
of the nature of your kingdom,
and help us to live accordingly.
Teach us that the treasures you give,
whether earthly or heavenly,
are not to be hoarded,
stashed away for our own benefit,
but to be shared,
consecrated back to you in your service
and to the benefit of others.
Grant us, then, generosity of spirit
and spontaneity in devotion,
so that we will understand the true meaning of riches
and be ready to give as freely as we have received,
through Jesus Christ our Lord.
Amen.

Nick Fawcett

Psalm 49

Come, one and all, from near and far,
to share the insights I have found:
a heart which has been taught by faith
informs the wisdom I expound.

Some flaunt their gold, some trust its power –
but what they cherish will decay;
and still the ransom for a soul
remains a price too great to pay.

Though wealth or learning may be ours,
or fame that spreads throughout the land,
the shackles of mortality
prevent so much that we have planned.

Beyond this age of shame and sham
we glimpse a better destiny:
the Lord will lift us free from death
to walk with him eternally.

Why crave renown or opulence?
They fade, those things we now possess;
our hope, our life are in the Lord,
the God we honour and confess.

Martin E. Leckebusch

Metre: 88 88 (LM)
Suggested tune: *Bow Brickhill*

Proper 14

Year A

Genesis 37:1-4, 12-28
or 1 Kings 19:9-18
Psalm 105:1-6, 16-22, 45b
or Psalm 85:8-13
Romans 10:5-15
Matthew 14:22-33

You of little faith, why did you doubt? (Matthew 14:31b)

Prayer

Blessed are you, Lord our God,
for you are a very present help in trouble.
You are ready to hear our cry
and come to our aid.
Lord, help us not to be afraid
but to put our trust and hope in you.
May we ever rejoice in your love and care.
Blessed are you, Father, Son and Holy Spirit,
one God for ever.

Lord, you have created us out of love
and for your love.
We ask for your protection
in the troubles and storms of life.
Bless all Christians who are struggling against
great odds.
We pray for those who are suffering
from persecution, violence or ridicule.
We remember those whose lives are at risk
and those who are exhausted.

Lord, in the storms of life,
hear us and help us.
Amen.

David Adam

Poem

For thinking I can ever know
the way you have things planned,
forgetting that I need to grow
if I would understand;
for feeling you can be contained
by my poor reach of mind,
assuming truth can be explained
or rigidly defined;
for all the ways my faith is flawed
and understanding skewed,
I ask your pardon, gracious Lord,
and beg to be renewed.

Nick Fawcett

Proper 14

Year B

2 Samuel 18:5-9, 15, 31-33
   or 1 Kings 19:4-8
Psalm 130
   or Psalm 34:1-8
Ephesians 4:25 – 5:2
John 6:35, 41-51

I am the bread of life. (John 6:48)

Prayer

Blessed are you, Lord our God,
for you provided for your children.
In the wilderness of this world
you give us the bread of life.
Lord, grant, as we journey towards the Promised Land,
that we may put our hope and our trust in you.
Blessed are you, Father, Son and Holy Spirit.

Father, we give you thanks that you have called us
to know you and to love you.
You have drawn us to you with bands of love.
Help us to listen and to obey your word.
We pray for all preachers and pastors,
for ministers of the word and of the sacraments.
We remember before you all who do not know or love you
and we ask your blessing upon all
who reach out in mission and love to them.
We pray for any who have lost faith in themselves or in you.

Lord our God,
our hope is in you.
Amen.

David Adam

Hymn

You are the Bread of Life
which feeds the hungry soul;
your body, broken on the cross,
was torn to make us whole.
Your flesh is food so real,
your blood is drink indeed –
Lord Jesus, in your life we find
the nourishment we need.

You are the Prince of Peace,
the one who offers rest
for troubles, weary, aching hearts
by burdens long oppressed.
You will not weigh us down,
our load you humbly bear –
how glad we are to learn your ways,
your easy yoke to share.

You are the only Way,
the Truth whom we believe,
and those who place their trust in you
eternal life receive.
You make the Father known,
his glory lights your face –
his splendour you reveal to us
in mercy, truth and grace.

Martin E. Leckebusch

Metre: DSM
Suggested tune: *Diademata*

Proper 14

Year C

Isaiah 1:1, 10-20
or Genesis 15:1-6
Psalm 50:1-8, 23, 24
or Psalm 33:12-22
Hebrews 11:1-3, 8-16
Luke 12:32-40

Where your treasure is, there your heart will be also. (Luke 12:34)

Prayer

Blessed are you, Lord our God,
for you have called us to know you
and to love you.
You, Lord, are our strength and our shield,
our protector and our joy.
Blessed are you, Father, Son and Holy Spirit.

Lord, in your power
may your Church be a place of peace for the anxious
and a stronghold for all who are troubled.
We ask your blessing
upon all who are involved in pastoral work
and in caring for others.
We pray for the Church's ministry
to the outcasts and marginalised people of society.

Powerful God,
protect us and give us your peace.
Amen.

David Adam

Poem

If you ever get to heaven,
you'll be shown around
by a guardian angel.
And one of the places you'll visit
on the very first day
will be the Celestial Bank.
(I know there is a bank,
because Jesus told us
to lay up treasures for ourselves
in heaven.)
So they'll bring out your account,
and with a frown and a sigh
and a shaking of the head
they'll probably say,
'If only you'd put more in
on earth,
you could have taken more out
in heaven.'

So be warned –
it isn't yet too late
to start investing.

Peter Dainty

Proper 15

Year A

Genesis 45:1-15
    or Isaiah 56:1, 6-8
Psalm 133
    or Psalm 67
Romans 11:1-2a, 29-32
Matthew 15:(10-20) 21-28

My house shall be called a house of prayer for all peoples. (Isaiah 56:7c)

Prayer

Blessed are you, Lord our God,
for you have created us all out of love
and for your love.
Even when in our sin and foolishness
we go against you and leave you,
you are there and seek us out in love.
Blessed are you, Father, Son and Holy Spirit.

Loving God,
may your Church throughout the world
show your love for all peoples and nations.
Bless all who seek to heal divisions
and to do away with prejudice.
Give courage to all who reach out to those in need
and who seek to welcome the rejected.
May your Church reflect your saving love.

Lord of life and love,
hear us and help us.
Amen.

David Adam

Psalm 67

May God be gracious, granting us his favour,
shining on us the kindness of his face,
so that his sovereign purpose of salvation
may stand revealed to all the human race.

May all the peoples lift their hearts in worship;
may every nation bring its joyful song;
may they exalt the God who guides and judges,
upholding right and overturning wrong.

Then shall the earth rejoice in God's abundance –
more than enough for every nation's need!
When all the peoples honour his intentions,
then shall we know God's gracious touch indeed.

Martin E. Leckebusch

Metre: 11 10 11 10
Suggested tune: *Lord of the Years*

Proper 15

Year B

1 Kings 2:10-12; 3:3-14
or Proverbs 9:1-6
Psalm 111
or Psalm 34:9-14
Ephesians 5:15-20
John 6:51-58

Wisdom 'calls from the highest places in town'. (Proverbs 9:3b)

Prayer

Grant me grace, Lord, to be strong and wise in all things. Give me a generous love. Fill me with the spirit of intelligence and wisdom. Let me always be mindful of others. O perfect and eternal Light, enlighten me.

Alcuin of York

Hymn

How rich and deep God's judgements are,
his knowledge, how profound!
Who understands the path he takes?
His wisdom, who can sound?
If we should try to guide his thoughts
no counsel could we find
to offer the all-seeing One
who forms both heart and mind.

And who can give him anything
which he must then repay,
or charge a debt to his account
against the judgement day?
Eternal glory and renown
shall evermore be his –
the Source of all created things,
the End of all that is!

And yet our living sacrifice
this awesome God desires:
our mortal bodies, yielded up,
to serve as he requires!
Such giving is a sacred act,
such worship, pure and right:
the best response of thankful hearts,
and pleasing in his sight.

Then by his all-surpassing power
our minds he will transform
to see this world's ungodly ways
no longer as the norm:
for hearts and lives renewed by grace
at last can truly learn
God's good and pleasing will to prove,
his judgements to discern.

Martin E. Leckebusch

Metre: 8 6 8 6 D (DCM)
Suggested tune: *Kingsfold*

Proper 15

Year C

Isaiah 5:1-7
  or Jeremiah 23:23-29
Psalm 80:1, 2, 9-20
  or Psalm 82
Hebrews 11:29 – 12:2
Luke 12:49-56

Give justice to the weak and the orphan. (Psalm 82:3a)

Prayer

Living God,
reveal to us more of your will
and equip us to honour it.
Save us from taking the path of least resistance,
opting for peace where there is no peace
or pretending all is well when the reality is
  otherwise.
Give us instead the faith and courage we need
to stand up for what is right,
even if that risks alienating people,
including, perhaps, those we love.
Hear us and help us, O God,
in the name of Christ.
Amen.

Nick Fawcett

Psalm 82

The cry is heard from heaven:
the Judge presides in court!
He questions our integrity
by judgements we distort.

The voiceless, powerless poor
are harassed to despair;
their welfare is God's charge to us;
their cause is ours to share.

But those who rule this world
choose wilful ignorance,
till all creation quakes in shame
before such insolence.

For holy dignity
the human race was made;
but mortal nature, flawed by sin,
leaves hearts and hopes betrayed.

The cry goes up to heaven:
'Lord, make your justice known,
for all the earth is yours to judge,
and every land, your own.'

Martin E. Leckebusch

Metre: 66 86 (SM)
Suggested tune: *Carlisle*

Proper 16

Year A

Exodus 1:8 – 2:10
  or Isaiah 51:1-6
Psalm 124
  or Psalm 138
Romans 12:1-8
Matthew 16:13-20

You are the Messiah, the Son of the living God. (Matthew 16:16)

Prayer

Loving Lord,
once more we would confess our faith in you,
acknowledging you as the Messiah,
the Son of the living God,
the one who sets us free and brings us life.
Help us to honour you not only in words
but also through living faithfully as your people,
your Body,
your Church,
working for and witnessing to your kingdom
  in word and deed.
Receive our worship,
receive our faith,
for your name's sake.
Amen.

Nick Fawcett

Psalm 138

What faithfulness, Lord, and what love you have
  shown!
My heart overflows as I bow at your throne;
no matter who hears me, nor what they believe,
I pour out my worship for you to receive.

Unparalleled honours belong to your name;
your word is exalted, unrivalled in fame:
that word was the message I needed to hear –
I prayed, and you helped me to conquer my fear.

Let all in authority listen to you
and lift up the offering of praise you are due:
for though you are far from those captive to pride,
you come to the lowly and walk by their side.

You hold me through trouble, secure in your
  hand:
my foes cannot rob me of what you have planned.
Lord, safe in your keeping, allow me to prove
your unfailing purpose, your unfailing love.

Martin E. Leckebusch

Metre: 11 11 11 11
Suggested tune: *Stowey*

Proper 16

Year B

1 Kings 8:(1, 6, 10, 11) 22-30, 41-43
or Joshua 24:1-2a, 14-18
Psalm 84
or Psalm 34:15-22
Ephesians 6:10-20
John 6:56-69

Take up the whole armour of God. (Ephesians 6:13a)

Prayer

Blessed are you, Lord our God;
in you is life and life eternal.
You love us with an everlasting love.
You give us the freedom to turn to you or turn away from you.
You do not compel us to love you
but invite us to know you and your love.
Help us in our desire to know you
and to be more faithful to you.
Blessed are you, God, for ever.

We give you thanks for all your faithful people.
We rejoice in the fellowship of your saints
and all who have been loyal to you.
We remember before you those who are new to the faith
and all who are seeking to deepen their faith.
We pray for all who are tempted to turn their back on you,
those who are troubled by doubt
and all those who are finding their faith a challenge.

Holy Lord,
our trust is in you.
Amen.

David Adam

Poem

Christian soldiers in the fight
wrestling evil forces,
great are our resources!
Mighty armour God provides:
using every section
gives us full protection.

As a belt we take the truth,
trusting God to save us
by the truth he gave us.
What a breastplate: God himself
tells us how he sees us –
righteous in Christ Jesus!

Now we wear the gospel shoes,
everywhere declaring
peace that is for sharing;
when we raise the shield of faith
how can Satan harm us?
He will not alarm us!

Gift of God to bring our minds
into liberation:
helmet of salvation!
Such a powerful sword to wield:
how God's word inspires us!
How his Spirit fires us!

When we pray, the Spirit's voice
whispers deep inside us,
speaking words to guide us:
God has pledged to bring us through,
in his strength abounding –
all our foes confounding!

Martin E. Leckebusch

Proper 16

Year C

Jeremiah 1:4-10
or Isaiah 58:9b-14
Psalm 7:1-6
or Psalm 103:1-8
Hebrews 12:18-29
Luke 13:10-17

You shall be like a watered garden, like a spring of water, whose waters never fail.
(Isaiah 58:11b)

Prayer

Blessed are you, Lord our God,
for you sent your Son to set us free
from sin and death.
You offer us the glorious liberty
of the children of God.
Help us to reveal your love and your freedom
in the way we live and deal with each other.
Blessed are you Father, Son and Holy Spirit.
Amen.

David Adam

Poem

Though I have known from childhood
that many tiny flowerets
grow in our dear Lord's garden,
it is only recently
that I came across a copy
of the Lord's seed catalogue;
and these are some of the varieties
I found within its pages.

Suburbiana Respectabilia
This respectable climber
grows well
in pleasant conditions
and with the help
of a suitable
adjacent building.
Plant in September
and it will blossom at Christmas
and, with sufficient care,
bear fruit by Easter.
Then it rests until Autumn.
It does not easily
survive transplanting.

Grandioso Ritualis
This dressy plant,
which flourishes, surprisingly,
in a smoky atmosphere,
produces flowers of different colours
for every season of the year.
It is at its best in clusters,
which enhance its stately presence,
and its solemn dignity
will grace any occasion.

Hierarchico Administrasis
This pot plant flourishes behind glass,
especially office windows,
where it proliferates
with minimum attention
or encouragement.
The main problem is
to keep its growth
within reasonable bounds.
It bears an abundance
of papery fruit
all year round,
most of which is
entirely lacking in nutritional value.

Mystico Solitaris
This stark, cactus-like plant
grows well in desert conditions –
the more severe the conditions,
the more fragrant the flowers.
Its fruit is only valued
by those who are lost
in the wilderness.
To others, it has a bitter taste.

Saint
A humble plant
which grows in any situation,
and has been found hidden
among all the plants described above.
Its simple beauty
has the strange effect
of bringing out the best
in those around it,
and its sweet aroma
fills the air with a sense
of calm and goodwill.

Peter Dainty, adapted

Proper 17
Year A

Exodus 3:1-15
  or Jeremiah 15:15-21
Psalm 105:1-6, 23-26, 45b
  or Psalm 26:1-8
or Psalm 115
Romans 12:9-21
Matthew 16:21-28

Remove the sandals from your feet, for the place on which you are standing is holy ground. (Exodus 3:5)

Prayer

Lord Jesus Christ,
we want to honour you by living as your disciples
and walking in your way,
but we find it hard,
our inclinations so very different to your own.
Reveal to us, we pray,
more of what it means to follow you,
more about the true nature of discipleship.
Help us to grasp the meaning of your kingdom,
where losers are winners,
the first are last,
and those who lose their life for your sake will
  truly find it.
Teach us now,
by your grace.
Amen.

Nick Fawcett

Poem

The bush that burns and dies
  is not of God.
When its blazing turns to ashes,
  and its momentary glory
  smokes to an unsensational ending;
when today's bright star
  falls into the cold night
  of yesterday's headlines;
when the man of the hour
  withers in the heat
  of his short-lived fame;
when the whiz kid skids into oblivion;
when the passionate movement,
  born in fervour,
  dies of over-exposure
  in the bitter winds of change;
when the state smell rises
  from the burnt-out fag end
  of a passing fashion;
when the bush dies with its burning,
  then you know
  that it is not of God.

But where the bush burns
  and is not consumed,
  there is God.
Where sparks of faith
  explode in a dark age;
where martyrs' eyes
  gleam bright with hope;
where prophets' words
  shine through the mocking night;
where flames of love
  will not be quenched by hate;
where strugglers radiate joy
  and saints die on their knees;
where Christ's truth
  shines fresh in each new age;
where the bush burns
  and is not consumed,
  then you know
  that there is God.

Peter Dainty

Proper 17

Year B

Song of Solomon 2:8-13
or Deuteronomy 4:1, 2, 6-9
Psalm 45:1, 2, 6-9
or Psalm 15
James 1:17-27
Mark 7:1-8, 14, 15, 21-23

Honour those who fear the Lord. (Psalm 15:4b)

Prayer

Almighty God,
help us truly to worship you –
to offer not superficial show,
empty piety,
lifeless ritual
or outward observance,
but heartfelt praise,
true thanksgiving,
genuine penitence,
sacrificial commitment,
meaningful intercession
and a real hunger and thirst
to know and serve you better.
Work within us now,
so that what we declare with our lips
we may believe in our hearts
and display in our lives,
to your glory.
Amen.

Nick Fawcett

Psalm 15

Lord, I approach your sanctuary –
but as I come to seek your face
the challenges of holiness
confront me in this sacred place.

Your searchlight falls across my path –
what flaws and failures will it show?
Am I content to speak the truth,
to slander neither friend nor foe?

Esteem for those who savour sin,
disdain for those who fear your name –
Lord, if such attitudes are mine,
then I deserve to suffer shame.

If I neglect some costly pledge,
or let a bribe distort my sight,
or simply disregard the poor –
convict me, Lord, of wrong and right.

Give me a single-minded faith,
an eager ear for your command;
make mine a life securely built
on solid rock, not shifting sand.

Martin E. Leckebusch

Metre: 88 88 (LM)
Suggested tune: *Fulda*

Proper 17

Year C

Jeremiah 2:4-13
  or Ecclesiasticus 10:12-18
  or Proverbs 25:6, 7
Psalm 81:1, 10-16
  or Psalm 112
Hebrews 13:1-8, 15, 16
Luke 14:1, 7-14

When you give a banquet, invite the poor, the crippled, the lame, and the blind.
(Luke 14:13)

Prayer

Blessed are you, Lord our God,
for you come to us in love and with blessings.
You are to be met in our encounters
with friends and with strangers
as you are in all and about all.
Blessed are you, Father, Son and Holy Spirit.

We give thanks that you have called us to know you
and ask that we may always serve you faithfully.
Bless all who are called to preach the word
and administer the sacraments.
We pray for all who are training for ministry
and all who are seeking to understand and
  proclaim your word.

Lord God Almighty,
hear us and help us.
Amen.

David Adam

Psalm 112

Joy comes to those who have trusted you, Lord,
  for salvation,
those who obey your commands with unfeigned
  adoration.
This is our prayer:
  make us more fully aware
holiness is our vocation.

Joy comes to those who have brought up their
  children to fear you,
joy to observe how they live by the truth and revere
  you.
This is our prayer,
  Lord, for those under our care:
may they be constantly near you.

Joy comes to those who find bountiful giving a
  pleasure,
those who seek justice and kindness as riches to
  treasure.
This is our prayer:
  Lord, make us eager to share;
make your compassion our measure.

Joy comes to those who are sure they will not be
  forsaken,
those with no malice that life with its pains might
  awaken.
This is our prayer:
  when those who scorn you despair,
Lord, let our faith be unshaken.

Martin E. Leckebusch

Metre: 14 14 4 7 8
Suggested tune: *Lobe den Herren*

Proper 18

Year A

Exodus 12:1-14
or Ezekiel 33:7-11
Psalm 149
or Psalm 119:33-40
Romans 13:8-14
Matthew 18:15-20

Where two or three are gathered in my name, I am there among them.
(Matthew 18:20)

Prayer

Lord Jesus Christ,
you promise that where two or three are gathered
in your name,
you will be there in the midst of them,
and so we come now,
eager to meet with you:
to hear your voice,
receive your guidance,
offer our worship
and do your will.
Come among us through your Spirit
and help us to sense your nearness.
Fill our hearts and minds,
so that when we return to the daily business of life
we will know you are with us there too
and be equipped to walk in your way,
faithful and true to our journey's end.
Amen.

Nick Fawcett

Poem

(*For up to six readers.*)

Lord, you are all around us.
Open our eyes to see –
in star and mountain, sun and snow;
in ocean, flower and tree.

Lord, you are all around us.
Help us to understand –
in speech and music, book and poem;
in artist's brush and hand.

Lord, you are all around us.
Give us the faith to know –
in prayer and worship, bread and wine;
in cross and candle glow.

Lord, you are all around us.
Fill us with love to care –
for friends and family, stranger and foe;
our neighbours everywhere.

Lord, you are deep within us.
Move us to live for you –
give strength and courage, hope and peace,
in all that we are and do.

Lord, you are close beside us.
Lead us in paths of right –
through joy and sorrow, laughter and tears,
journeying to the light.

Peter Dainty

Proper 18

Year B

Proverbs 22:1, 2, 8, 9, 22, 23
or Isaiah 35:4-7a
Psalm 125
or Psalm 146
James 2:1-10 (11-13) 14-17
Mark 7:24-37

You shall love your neighbour as yourself. (James 2:8)

Prayer

Blessed are you, Lord our God,
for you have called your people
from every tribe, nation and language.
We rejoice that you care for all peoples
and every single individual
and seek to offer each of them your love.
You have called us all to hear your word
and to proclaim your praises.
Blessed are you, Father, Son and Holy Spirit.

We rejoice that your Church is for all people
in all times and in all places.
No one who comes to you is cast out.
May we seek to make your Church open
and welcoming to all.
We ask your blessing upon all who are involved
in the outreach and mission of the church.
We remember especially those who seek
to proclaim your love by word and example.
We pray for all who have not heard of you
and your saving grace.

God, ever with us,
be our strength and our Saviour.
Amen.

David Adam

Poem

Lord, for using labels to decide on people's worth:
their age, their sex, their class, their roots,
their faith or place of birth,
their politics or culture, the colour of their skin,
the outward signs that mark them out
instead of what's within;
for summing people up by what nobody can
change –
allowing background, creed or race
to poison and estrange –
for all such prejudice, forgive, and from it set me free
to meet the person underneath –
to look and really see.

Nick Fawcett

Proper 18

Year C

Jeremiah 18:1-11
or Deuteronomy 30:15-20
Psalm 139:1-5, 12-18
or Psalm 1
Philemon 1-21
Luke 14:25-33

Just like the clay in the potter's hand, so are you in my hand, O house of Israel. (Jeremiah 18:6b)

Prayer

Lord Jesus,
I give you my hands to do your work.
I give you my feet to go your way.
I give you my eyes to see as you do.
I give you my tongue to speak your words.
I give you my mind that you may think in me.
I give you my spirit that you may pray in me.

Above all,
I give you my heart that you may love in me,
your Father, and all mankind.
I give you my whole self that you may grow in me,
so that it is you, Lord Jesus,
who live and work and pray in me.

I hand over to your care, Lord,
my soul and body,
my mind and thoughts,
my prayers and my hopes,
my health and my work,
my life and my death,
my parents and my family,
my friends and my neighbours,
my country and all men.
Today
and always.

Lancelot Andrewes

Poem

What do you do
with the broken pieces, Lord?
The coat with crooked seams,
the pot that cracked,
the bankrupt business,
and the broken heart?
Is there for you
a point of no return
or are these somewhere
set apart, recycled
and redeemed?
Somehow, I dream
of offering to you, Lord,
all that is smudged, spilled,
blasted and blasphemed,
that by your perfectness
they, too, may be restored.

Elizabeth Rooney

Proper 19

Year A

Exodus 14:19-31
 or Genesis 50:15-21
Psalm 114
 or *Canticle:* Exodus 15:1b-11, 20, 21
 or Psalm 103:(1-7) 8-13
Romans 14:1-12
Matthew 18:21-35

The Israelites went into the sea on dry ground, the waters forming a wall for them on their right and on their left. (Exodus 14:22)

Prayer

Gracious God,
we praise you that you welcome us into your presence
despite all that is unworthy in our lives:
all our faults, failing, falsehoods and faithlessness.
Speak to us through your willingness to forgive and go on forgiving,
and so help us to forgive in turn,
striving to heal broken relationships,
mend quarrels,
let bygones be bygones
and start afresh.
Teach us through the example of Christ
to show something of the mercy you have shown to us.
In his name we pray.
Amen.

Nick Fawcett

Poem

When the people looked behind them
and saw Pharaoh's hosts draw near,
they turned to prophet Moses,
and cried out in their fear:
'We were better off in Egypt,
we were better off as slaves,
than buried in the desert sand
or drowned in the Red Sea's waves.
If freedom can offer us nothing but death
what is it worth, we say?
Let us return to the life that we knew
in the land of yesterday.'

Then Moses said to the people,
'Stand firm, and don't be afraid;
the Lord who has brought us this far
will surely come to our aid.
The Egyptians you see behind you
may look like unbeatable men,
but when the Lord has done his work
you'll never see them again.
You've only just tasted the freedom of God,
you haven't yet had your fill.
Trust in the Lord who is with us today –
you only have to be still.'

But then the Lord said to Moses,
'Why do my people cry out?
They know the way I've led them,
so why do they stand and doubt?
Forget the false memories of Egypt;
it wasn't as good as they say.
Face up to the call of the future.
Go forward! There's no other way.'
So Moses walked down to the edge of the sea;
at God's word, he stretched out his hand.
A wind from the east blew the waters right back
and the people went through on dry land.

To live in the past is to live with the dead,
to be captives of things that have gone.
But tomorrow is full of the promise of God
and today is our chance to move on.

Peter Dainty

Proper 19

Year B

Proverbs 1:20-33
or Isaiah 50:4-9a
Psalm 19
or *Canticle:* Wisdom of Solomon 7:26 – 8:1
or Psalm 116:1-8
James 3:1-12
Mark 8:27-38

The law of the Lord is perfect, reviving the soul. (Psalm 19:7a)

Prayer

Govern everything by your wisdom, O Lord, so that my soul may always be serving you, in the way you will and not as I choose. Let me die to myself so that I may serve you; let me live to you, who are life itself. Amen.

St Teresa of Avila

Hymn

Amid the clamour of the world
the voice of God is heard:
the ear that has been taught by faith
can recognise his word.

For through the chequered history
of this rebellious race
obliquely, using human tongues,
the Lord has promised grace.

And yet to speak more plainly still
he made our life his own:
most clearly in the Son of Man
the Word of God is known.

He still reveals the truth to all
who truly want to learn –
who in their life-experience
the hand of God discern.

This is no mere philosophy,
but all the tools of life;
his Spirit speaks the holy word
in all our joy and strife.

Equip us, Lord, to face the needs
confronting us today
with wisdom to perceive your call
and courage to obey.

Martin E. Leckebusch

Metre: 8 6 8 6 (CM)
Suggested tune: *Albano*

Proper 19
Year C

Jeremiah 4:11, 12, 22-28
or Exodus 32:7-14
Psalm 14
or Psalm 51:1-11
1 Timothy 1:12-17
Luke 15:1-10

Rejoice with me, for I have found the coin that I had lost. (Luke 15:9)

Prayer

Lord Jesus Christ,
in the knowledge that you love us enough to seek us out,
however often we go astray,
that you are always ready to welcome us back,
eager to forgive and forget,
so we come now, summoned by your love,
despite having erred and strayed like lost sheep,
disobeying your will
and rejecting your guidance in so much.
We come in penitence,
but also assurance,
knowing that you welcome us joyfully
and without reserve.
Teach us, we pray, as we worship now,
to value you as much as you value us.
Amen.

Nick Fawcett

Psalm 51

Have mercy on me, loving Lord,
for I have sinned so much:
in your compassion let me feel
your gracious, cleansing touch.

My many sins I know too well;
I find your verdict true:
throughout my life my inmost thoughts
have seldom honoured you.

Create in me a willingness
to leave those things behind –
and may the joy your Spirit brings
sustain my heart and mind.

Then I shall tell my neighbours, too,
where mercy can be found,
till others turn to you in faith,
and hymns of praise resound.

For contrite hearts are your delight –
what more do you require?
The offerings born of brokenness
are all that you desire.

Martin E. Leckebusch

Metre: 86 86 (CM)
Suggested tunes: *St Fulbert; St Gilbert (Elizabeth Hill)*

Proper 20

Year A

Exodus 16:2-15
  or Jonah 3:10 – 4:11
Psalm 105:1-6, 37-45
  or Psalm 145:1-8
Philippians 1:21-30
Matthew 20:1-16

The last will be first, and the first will be last. (Matthew 20:16)

Prayer

Sovereign and saving God,
for your mercy that redeems us
and your love that welcomes us
we praise you.
We deserve nothing
and yet you gave all to bring us life,
now and always.
Help us today to grasp the extent of your love,
the breadth of your purpose
and the scope of your grace –
to recognise that no one is beyond your mercy
or outside your concern.
Teach us, then,
to be generous in our dealings with others,
as you have dealt so generously with us,
through Jesus Christ our Lord.
Amen.

Nick Fawcett

Psalm 145

Let us exalt our King,
  offer our finest praise;
daily, and evermore,
  let us applaud his ways!
How right that he should be adored –
our great, unfathomable Lord.

Tell of his majesty,
  splendours of dazzling light;
speak of the awesome power
  shown in his acts of might!
As on these things we meditate,
how can we help but celebrate?

Under his gracious reign
  mercy will never fail;
anger is seldom found,
  kindness and love prevail:
his kingdom ever will endure,
a realm eternally secure.

Promises made – and kept;
  love which embraces all;
strength for the weary heart,
  courage for those who fall –
our God provides what each requires;
he loves to meet our hearts' desires.

Let us exalt our King,
  serve him in godly fear –
trusting his saving power,
  conscious that he is near.
How right it is to spread his fame!
Let every being praise his name!

Martin E. Leckebusch

Metre: 66 66 88
Suggested tune: *Little Cornard*

Proper 20

Year B

Proverbs 31:10-31
 or Wisdom of Solomon
 1:16 – 2:1, 12-22
 or Jeremiah 11:18-20
Psalm 1
 or Psalm 54
James 3:13 – 4:3, 7-8a
Mark 9:30-37

Whoever welcomes one such child in my name welcomes me. (Mark 9:37a)

Prayer

Lord Jesus Christ,
Lord of all yet servant of all,
teach us your way of gentleness and humility,
so that we in turn may serve you and others.
Nurture us now, as we worship you,
and put a new nature within us –
a childlike innocence and sincerity,
enthusiasm and spontaneity,
trust and dependence –
so that, open to fresh horizons,
we may be ready to learn more of you,
to grow in grace,
and to respond obediently to your call in faith
 and love,
to your glory.
Amen.

Nick Fawcett

Poem

Save me from empty pleas, Lord,
from prayers that are short on deeds,
from claiming to care for others
but ignoring their basic needs.
Save me from false religion
through which souls alone are fed –
from faith that offers the gospel
yet forgets to give daily bread.
Fill me with Christ's compassion,
inspire me freely to give,
to share with joy from my plenty
that others might simply live.

Nick Fawcett

Proper 20

Year C

Jeremiah 8:18 – 9:1
or Amos 8:4-7
Psalm 79:1-9
or Psalm 113
1 Timothy 2:1-7
Luke 16:1-13

The children of this age are more shrewd in dealing with their own generation than are the children of light. (Luke 16:8b)

Prayer

Lord God,
speak to us again of the things in life that really matter,
that offer true joy and lasting fulfilment,
for we so easily and often forget.
Remind us that the riches of this world
can sometimes possess *us* rather than us *them*,
and teach us, then, to use them wisely and generously,
setting our hearts above all on treasures in heaven –
the blessings of joy, hope, love and peace,
life in abundance that you alone can offer.
Open our lives now to receive and respond,
through Jesus Christ our Lord.
Amen.

Nick Fawcett

Poem

They've converted our church
into a car showroom.
Jesus has been driven from his Temple
by the moneychangers
and car salesmen.
But the children of mammon
have proved more skilled
in attracting the eye
of the passer-by
than the children of light;
for the flashing neon,
is more appealing
than the peeling noticeboard.
The grimy stained-glass angels
have returned to heaven
and this worldy Temple
is now filled
with gleaming, metallic chariots
promising power, freedom and delight.
The sticky brown pews,
rigidly going nowhere,
have been replaced
by the luxurious leather
of long-distance limousines;
and all those sleepy sermons
have given way
to the restrained excitement
of solemn sales talk;
while the refurbished vestry
bears hushed witness
to the ritual signing
of new covenants,
opening the road
to a mechanical promised land
by easy payments.

The old harmonium's drone
has been silenced
by the subtle murmur
of piped music;
and glossy brochures,
not brown-leaved hymnals,
sing the praises
of god the machine.

Yet over the entrance,
indelibly carved in stone,
these words can still be read –
'The earth is the Lord's,
and the fullness thereof;
the world,
and they that dwell therein.'

Peter Dainty

Proper 21
Year A

Exodus 17:1-7
    or Ezekiel 18:1-4, 25-32
Psalm 78:1-4, 12-16
    or Psalm 25:1-8
Philippians 2:1-13
Matthew 21:23-32

At the name of Jesus every knee should bend. (Philippians 2:10)

Prayer

Lord Jesus Christ,
teach us to recognise your authority in our lives
and to respond freely to your call.
Show us what you would have us do
and how you would have us serve.
Though the way may be hard
and our inclination be to resist,
inspire us, through love of you, to obey your summons
and honour your will.
Above all, help us each day to recognise our need of you,
and to receive again the love and pardon you delight to give.
We come now,
hearts open in faith,
lives offered in love,
to your glory.
Amen.

Nick Fawcett

Hymn

All power to the Lamb of God:
he wore the robes of servanthood
and in the place of weakness stood –
all power to the Lamb!

All riches to the Lamb of God
who came among us, one so poor,
to make us rich for evermore –
all riches to the Lamb!

All wisdom to the Lamb of God
who chose the way of suffering:
to status he refused to cling –
all wisdom to the Lamb!

And to the Lamb of God, all strength:
his love was strong enough to win,
defeating all the might of sin –
and to the Lamb, all strength!

All honour to the Lamb of God
who laid his honour far aside
when on a cross of shame he died –
all honour to the Lamb!

All glory to the Lamb of God:
his name above all others now;
let every knee before him bow –
all glory to the Lamb!

All praises to the Lamb of God,
for he is worthy, who was slain,
who now and evermore shall reign –
all praises to the Lamb!

Martin E. Leckebusch

Metre: 8 88 6
Suggested tunes: *Misericordia; Saffron Walden*

Proper 21

Year B

Esther 7:1-6, 9, 10; 9:20-22
  or Numbers 11:4-6, 10-16, 24-29
Psalm 124
  or Psalm 19:7-14
James 5:13-20
Mark 9:38-50

We have escaped like a bird from the snare of the fowlers.
(Psalm 124:7a)

Prayer

Sovereign God,
we would draw close and learn of you,
so that we might know, love and serve you better.
Receive, then, the worship we bring
and meet us through it,
speaking your word,
offering your guidance,
imparting your strength
and granting your mercy.
Give us a clearer understanding of your will
and help us to recognise everything in our lives
that conspires against it;
that leads us astray,
separating us from you and one another.
Grant us grace to resist temptation,
and to walk in your way,
now and always.
Amen.

Nick Fawcett

Psalm 124

Unless the Lord had stood with us –
let all God's people say –
would not the angry storm we faced
have swept our lives away?

Had not the Lord defended us
from such a fierce attack,
who could have met those dreadful foes
and held the onslaught back?

But God, our God, has rescued us
from their brutality:
the fowler's snare is broken now,
the captive birds fly free.

The Maker of the galaxies,
the Lord of earth and heaven,
has promised all the help we need –
all praise to God be given!

Martin E. Leckebusch

Metre: 86 86 (CM)
Suggested tunes: *Irish; Kilmarnock*

Proper 21
Year C

Jeremiah 32:1-3a, 6-15
or Amos 6:1a, 4-7
Psalm 91:1-6, 14-16
or Psalm 146
1 Timothy 6:6-19
Luke 16:19-31

Father Abraham, have mercy on me . . . for I am in agony in these flames.
(Luke 16:24)

Prayer

Blessed are you, Lord our God,
for you have created us and supplied all we need.
You have created a world
where there is enough for everyone's need
but not for everyone's greed.
Teach us to live graciously as you are gracious to us.
Blessed are you, Father, Son and Holy Spirit.

God, we ask your blessing
upon your Church throughout the world,
that it may witness to your love
and your saving power.
We remember especially where the Church is
reaching out
to the extremely poor and the outcasts of society.
We ask you to guide
all who stand against injustice and oppression.
May your Church work for the liberation
of all who are used as slave labour
or who are in refugee camps.

God, we trust in you:
hear us and help us.
Amen.

David Adam

Poem

The rich man feasted all the day long,
while the poor man lay at his door.
The rich man's body was sleek and fat,
while the poor man's was thin and sore.
The rich man's clothes were costly and fine
but the poor man's were dirty and worn.
O save us, Lord, from this great divide
into which rich and poor are born.

May we who are rich learn to share our wealth
with the poor who lie at our gate;
and use our abundance for everyone's good,
before we discover too late
that the time has come when the great divide,
that separates rich from poor,
has become the divide between heaven and hell –
and we're the wrong side of the door.

Lord, help us to pull all the barriers down
that threaten our social health:
the walls of colour and sex and creed,
of nationhood and of wealth.
Prevent us from turning the human race
to a warring and cancerous cell,
which reduces the planet to nuclear dust
in the fires of a man-made hell.

We've failed to respond to your message of doom
in all that the prophets have said;
but now, in your mercy, you've sent us new hope,
through the preacher who rose from the dead.
May we hear his voice; may we follow his way;
may we learn what leads to peace;
may his beautiful Kingdom of justice and love
for ever and ever increase.

Peter Dainty

Proper 22

Year A

Exodus 20:1-4, 7-9, 12-20
  or Isaiah 5:1-7
Psalm 19
  or Psalm 80:8-16
Philippians 3:4b-14
Matthew 21:33-46

I press on towards the goal for the prize of the heavenly call of God in Christ Jesus.
(Philippians 3:14)

Prayer

Loving God,
help us, as we worship you,
to look honestly at ourselves
and recognise where we fail you,
where our lives fall short,
where our commitment is weak,
where the harvest is poor.
Come to us afresh,
and bring growth in grace,
fresh shoots of the Spirit,
signs of new life.
In your mercy, nurture our faith,
so that we might bear fruit for you,
reflecting your love
and living to your praise and glory,
through Jesus Christ our Lord.
Amen.

Nick Fawcett

Poem

Ahead of us, a race to run:
so, looking at the past no more,
forgetting what has gone before,
we fix our eyes on God the Son –
with eager diligence we train
as for the prize ahead we strain
until at last our course is done.

He calls us now to run the race,
discarding every weight and load
to speed our way along the road;
the path we tread, the way of grace –
and though the journey may be long
the grace of God will keep us strong
until we stand before his face.

Martin E. Leckebusch

Proper 22
Year B

Job 1:1; 2:1-10
  or Genesis 2:18-24
Psalm 26
  or Psalm 8
Hebrews 1:1-4 or 2:5-12
Mark 10:2-16

And the rib that the Lord God had taken from the man he made into a woman and brought her to the man. (Genesis 2:22)

Prayer

Living God,
through this time of worship
touch our being in every part:
our attitudes,
relationships,
thoughts, words and deeds;
the way we respond to you and others,
the way we love and live.
Teach us, in childlike humility,
to value all,
respect all
and work for the good of all,
recognising that everyone you have made is
  precious to you,
the work of your hands,
with a special place in your heart.
Reach out now
and put your Spirit within us,
through Jesus Christ our Lord,
Amen.

Nick Fawcett

Poem

Let Love rule in your lives,
and make you one.
Let Love rule everything –
all joys and pleasures,
and all grief and pain;
times of excitement and delight,
and the everyday routine.
Let Love rule in your minds,
that all your thoughts
be for the other's good,
and not their ill.
Let Love reign in your bodies,
so that you may share your passions
with an equal ecstasy,
but share them with no other.
And if Love truly reign within your hearts,
though trials come
which tempt you both to part,
you never will.
So let Love rule,
and you'll know then,
that I'll be with you both,
for evermore. Amen.

Peter Dainty

Proper 22
Year C

Lamentations 1:1-6
or Habakkuk 1:1-4; 2:1-4
Canticle: Lamentations 3:19-26
or Psalm 137
or Psalm 37:1-9
2 Timothy 1:1-14
Luke 17:5-10

How could we sing the Lord's song in a foreign land? (Psalm 137:4)

Prayer

Lord of all,
remind us today that you are a faithful and loving God,
a God who hears the cry of your people
and answers them in their distress.
Though you do not guarantee exemption
from pain, sorrow or hardship,
teach us that you promise always
to give us strength to meet adversity,
the inner presence of your Spirit
to encourage, comfort, equip and inspire,
bringing peace even in turmoil
and laughter even through tears.
Help us, then, to trust you whatever life brings,
through Jesus Christ our Lord.
Amen.

Nick Fawcett

Poem

By what surprising grace
did this lone prophet,
exiled in Babylon,
have the faith
to see the God of Israel
not as the defeated God
of a defeated people,
but as the Lord of all?

Did he not see around him
all the glory and the grandeur
that was Babylon –
the wealth and splendour
of her palaces and temples
and the famous gardens?
Was he not impressed
by all the pomp and dignity,
the might and majesty
of emperors and kings?
Did he not understand
that God's own Jerusalem
and holy sanctuary
were nothing now but dust,
while his decimated people
bowed in subjection
to a foreign law?
What miracle of faith
enabled him to see
the gods of Bablyon
as painted wooden idols
wobbling on their stands,
compared to Israel's living God,
whose breath shakes nations
and whose power compels the stars?

The ragged exiles
hung their harps upon the trees
and had no hearts for song;
but this lone, unnamed prophet
heard the music of the Lord
in an alien land,
and could not help but sing
of God's inevitable victory –
'Take comfort from your everlasting God,
he knows your plight; he comes to take you home.
He does not lack in power – he made the world!
He gives his strength to those who tire and fall.
And those who trust and wait will rise renewed.
They'll walk and run; on eagles' wings they'll soar.
For though the grass may wither, flowers fade,
the word of God endures for evermore.'

Peter Dainty

Proper 23

Year A

Exodus 32:1-14
or Isaiah 25:1-9
Psalm 106:1-6, 19-23
or Psalm 23
Philippians 4:1-9
Matthew 22:1-14

The Lord of hosts will make for all peoples a feast of rich food, a feast of well-matured wines. (Isaiah 25:6a)

Prayer

Living God,
we come at your invitation
to celebrate,
to receive,
to eat at your table and be filled.
Help us to prepare our hearts and minds
to receive all you offer
and to clothe ourselves with your gifts of love,
joy,
peace,
goodness,
compassion
and humility –
whatever is pleasing and honouring to you –
freely offering ourselves in the service of Christ,
who freely gave so much for us.
Amen.

Nick Fawcett

Hymn

God to whom all praise belongs,
God of excellence untold,
you declare that what is pure
has a greater worth than gold:
may the treasures you reveal
set my heart and mind aglow –
as your Spirit works in me
may the fruits of goodness grow.

God whose holy call I hear,
God whose words and ways are true,
may complete integrity
be the mark of all I do:
what can counter evil's guile
more than love's sincerity?
May the fruit of goodness grow
as your Spirit works in me.

God whose grace is mine to share,
God whose promise I believe,
all the fullness of your life
I am eager to receive.
Freed from sin's oppressive grasp,
more of you I long to know –
as your Spirit works in me
may the fruit of goodness grow.

God whose goodness never ends,
let my heart be yours alone;
tune my mind to think your thoughts,
mould my will to match your own;
let me show your righteousness
with untarnished clarity –
may the fruit of goodness grow
as your Spirit works in me.

Martin E. Leckebusch

Metre: 7 7 7 7 D
Suggested tunes: *Salzburg; Aberystwyth*

Proper 23

Year B

Job 23:1-9, 16, 17
  or Amos 5:6, 7, 10-15
Psalm 22:1-15
  or Psalm 90:12-17
Hebrews 4:12-16
Mark 10:17-31

It is easier for a camel to go through the eye of a needle than for someone who is rich to enter the kingdom of God. (Mark 10:25)

Prayer

Almighty God,
your word is unsettling,
demanding,
searching –
asking of us questions we'd rather not face,
summoning us to service that seems beyond us,
examining our innermost thoughts,
the intentions of the heart,
and calling for new beginnings,
radical change –
yet we need to hear it,
for we know also that it offers the way to life;
to peace, joy, hope and fulfilment,
both now and for all eternity.
So we approach you once more,
asking you to speak again and to help us listen,
that we might respond afresh
to your life-changing yet life-giving voice,
through Jesus Christ our Lord.
Amen.

Nick Fawcett

Poem

Let me boast in nothing but the cross
where the Lord was crucified;
I will place my pride in nothing else
but the cross where Jesus died.

On the cross he took what I deserved,
gave his life to set me free:
there he bore the judgement on my sin,
made himself accursed for me.
When I failed to live by God's commands
Jesus suffered in my place;
here I find the pardon which removes
both my guilt and my disgrace:

But the cross spells death for me as well:
I am crucified with Christ –
everything I used to be has died
since my Lord was sacrificed.
Now the key to life is faith in him,
since his promise I believe;
his unending resurrection life
is the gift I now receive:

So this world and I have parted now –
very different paths we take! –
all the worthless idols of this age
Christ commands me to forsake.
Earthly fame and riches cannot last,
neither will they satisfy;
at my Saviour's cross I take my stand,
and for him I live or die:

Martin E. Leckebusch

Proper 23

Year C

Jeremiah 29:1, 4-7
  or 2 Kings 5:1-3, 7-15c
Psalm 66:1-11
  or Psalm 111
2 Timothy 2:8-15
Luke 17:11-19

Get up and go on your way; your faith has made you well. (Luke 17:19)

Prayer

Sovereign God,
speak to us afresh through your word and this time of worship.
Help us, through standing in your presence,
to make sense of the changes and chances of this life –
the experiences that puzzle and bewilder,
the questions that baffle,
the facts that seem to undermine and even contradict our faith.
Though much may frustrate your purpose
and grieve your heart,
teach us that, through your great love and power,
you are able to turn sorrow to joy
and darkness to light,
somehow bringing good even out of evil.
In that faith may we trust you,
now and always,
in Jesus' name.
Amen.

Nick Fawcett

Poem

My nets are breaking, Lord.
I had not thought
to catch such an abundance
of your love.
So many years
I've toiled in my own strength
and taken nothing.

Now, suddenly, I'm filled
with you, your love,
your goodness, mercy, might.
You are my Lord, my love,
who gives me all delight.

Elizabeth Rooney

Proper 24

Year A

Exodus 33:12-23
or Isaiah 45:1-7
Psalm 99
or Psalm 96:1-9 (10-13)
1 Thessalonians 1:1-10
Matthew 22:15-22

Moses said, 'Show me your glory, I pray'. (Exodus 33:18)

Prayer

Lord of all,
teach us as citizens of heaven to live also as citizens of earth,
conducting ourselves in such a way as to bring honour to you.
Show us what it means to be your people in the daily business of life;
how best we might fulfil our responsibilities and duties to others
while staying true to you,
recognising your ultimate sovereignty over all.
Speak to us now,
and grant us the wisdom, sincerity and faith we need
to walk as your people,
within your world.
Amen.

Nick Fawcett

Psalm 99

Let every nation bow in godly fear
before the Lord whom angels all revere;
lift God's name high for all the world to hear –
holy is he!

Sing out his praise, this King of endless might
who shows his people what is just and right,
for righteousness and truth are his delight –
holy is he!

He gave the sacred law which Moses taught;
to him were Aaron's sacrifices brought;
this is the God whose favour Samuel sought –
holy is he!

This is our God, who hears and answers prayer,
who loathes our sin, but clears the guilt we hear;
before his throne, let heaven and earth declare;
holy is he!

Martin E. Leckebusch

Metre: 10 10 10 4
Suggested tunes: *Engleberg*

Proper 24

Year B

Job 38:1-7 (34-41)
or Isaiah 53:4-12
Psalm 104:1-10, 26, 35c
or Psalm 91:9-16
Hebrews 5:1-10
Mark 10:35-45

Whoever wishes to become great among you must be your servant. (Mark 10:44)

Prayer

Sovereign God,
teach us to follow you not for *our* ends but *yours*,
seeking first your glory and the furtherance of
your kingdom.
Remind us that the way of Christ
turns our understanding of life upside down,
freedom being found in service,
greatness in humility,
strength in weakness,
and life through dying to self.
Reveal to us more of what that means,
so that we might be equipped
to honour you here in our worship,
and each day in our lives,
through Jesus Christ our Lord.
Amen.

Nick Fawcett

Poem

Come and see what the Lord has revealed –
see a man so familiar with grief:
one whose face is disfigured and bruised,
one whose sufferings allow no relief.

See the anguish and woe that he bears –
what a burden to carry alone!
And we thought him afflicted by God,
never dreaming the load was our own.

See him pierced, see him crushed for our sin –
he was punished to bring us release:
we had all turned away from the truth;
he was scorned and abused for our peace.

And in silence he patiently stood
in the midst of oppression and strife:
for our hatred, our violence and lies
there he paid with the price of his life.

Yet the will of the Lord can be seen
in the painful ordeal he endured,
for the freedom his people enjoy
is the prize that his death has secured.

Come and see what the Lord has revealed –
see his Servant enthroned evermore,
for he poured out his life unto death
and the cost of salvation he bore.

Martin E. Leckebusch

Proper 24

Year C

Jeremiah 31:27-34
    or Genesis 32:22-31
Psalm 119:97-104
    or Psalm 121
2 Timothy 3:14 – 4:5
Luke 18:1-8

Will not God grant justice to his chosen ones who cry to him day and night? (Luke 18:7a)

Prayer

Blessed are you, Lord our God.
You are always more ready to hear than we are to pray,
and to grant more than we desire or deserve.
May we rejoice in your presence
and know your abiding love.
Blessed are you, Father, Son and Holy Spirit.

We give thanks for all who proclaim the Gospel,
especially those who risk their lives
or their comfort for your sake.
We ask you to bless all who preach the word,
theology students
and those who take part in Bible study groups.
We pray for those who meet quietly together
to pray and to contemplate your presence and your love.

Lord, hear us,
mercifully hear us.

We ask you to guide all who work in the judicial system.
We pray for law courts, judges, barristers, solicitors and juries.
We ask your blessing upon all
who seek to keep law and order.
We pray for the police
and for social workers and probation officers.
We remember all who suffer from injustice
and whose voices are not heard.

Lord, hear us,
mercifully hear us.
Amen.

David Adam

Poem

I stay at home,
cannot go out,
but all my prayers
go round about.

This one is blessed,
that one is healed.
What God will do
is not revealed
to me.
I just stay home
and pray.
God does the rest
in his own way.

Elizabeth Rooney

Proper 25

Year A

Deuteronomy 34:1-12
or Leviticus 19:1, 2, 15-18
Psalm 90:1-6, 13-17
or Psalm 1
1 Thessalonians 2:1-8
Matthew 22:34-46

Satisfy us in the morning with your steadfast love. (Psalm 90:14a)

Prayer

Sovereign God,
remind us through this time of worship of the essentials of faith –
love for you and love for others –
and through our being here today nurture such love within our lives.
Touch our hearts through your Spirit,
and renew us through the grace of Christ,
so that our devotion to you
and to the good of others
may be as real as that you so faithfully show us.
Help us now truly to love you
with heart and mind and soul,
and to love our neighbour as ourselves.
Amen.

Nick Fawcett

Poem

I offered songs of worship,
knelt down to you in prayer.
I sought your will and guidance,
and read your word with care.
I went to church each Sunday
and pledged to walk your way,
resolved to serve you better,
determined to obey.
To everyone around me,
I must have looked the part –
yet one thing, Lord, was lacking:
true worship from the heart.

Nick Fawcett

Proper 25

Year B

Job 42:1-6, 10-17
or Jeremiah 31:7-9
Psalm 34:1-8, 19-22
or Psalm 126
Hebrews 7:23-28
Mark 10:46-52

May those who sow in tears reap with shouts of joy. (Psalm 126:5)

Prayer

Blessed are you, Lord our God.
You created light out of darkness
and gave us eyes to see the beauty and wonders of your creation.
Lord, through the visible things of this world
lead us to see the invisible;
extend our vision beyond our eyes
that we may see with our hearts also.
Blessed are you, Father, Son and Holy Spirit.

We give thanks for the beauty and colour of our world,
for the gift of sight.
We ask your blessing upon men and women
who help us to see beyond the obvious,
upon all who are prophets and visionaries.
We pray for all who study your word
and who celebrate your sacraments.
We remember those training for ministry
and ask your blessing upon theological colleges
and all who teach Religious Education.

Lord, open our eyes
to see the invisible.
Amen.

David Adam

Poem

You are the giver of love,
holding my life in your hands,
filling my heart and feeding my soul,
granting your grace from above.

You are the giver of light,
shining on me and on all,
yearning to help and ready to guide,
bringing an end to the night.

You are the giver of joy,
aching to fill me with cheer,
making me glad and bringing delight,
bliss that no ill can destroy.

You are the giver of peace,
striving to make the world whole,
hungry to heal and thirsty to mend,
longing for hatred to cease.

You are the giver of all,
eager to bless me each day,
hands open wide, you freely impart
gifts to enrich and enthral.

Nick Fawcett

Proper 25

Year C

Joel 2:23-32
or Ecclesiasticus 35:12-17
or Jeremiah 14:7-10, 19-22
Psalm 65
or Psalm 84:1-7
2 Timothy 4:6-8, 16-18
Luke 18:9-14

All who exalt themselves will be humbled, but all who humble themselves will be exalted. (Luke 18:14b)

Prayer

Blessed are you, Lord God,
for in your grace and goodness
you have called us into life and to your love.
Though we are unworthy,
you accept us and love us.
Blessed are you, Father, Son and Holy Spirit.

Father, you hear the prayers of the lowly
and accept the penitent sinner.
Help your Church to welcome
all who seek forgiveness and newness of life.
Let us show how we all share
in your grace and goodness.
We pray for those who hear the confession of others
and for all who counsel those who are full of guilt and remorse.
May we all learn to trust in your love and acceptance.

Lord, hear us;
in your mercy hear us.
Amen.

David Adam

Hymn

Jesus, you have shown us how
to be humble, to be meek –
always tender, always kind,
neither compromised nor weak –
for your life and death alike
show the truth of all you spoke;
still, today, we hear your voice,
calling us to bear your yoke.

In our hearts we crown you King,
on our lips your name is heard,
and we willingly submit
to the teaching of your word –
so a trusted friend's rebuke
is a welcome blow indeed
when it leads us to the truth
and the discipline we need.

Let humility and grace
be the clothing that we wear
as in genuine concern
one another's load we bear.
May we love, and not condemn,
those who stumble, slip or fall;
let us help them once again
to receive your gracious call.

Though regarded by this world
with suspicion or disdain
still the meek enjoy your pledge:
all this earth they will obtain!
For the treasure in their hearts
has a value yet untold –
give us, Lord, that precious grace
which surpasses finest gold.

Martin E. Leckebusch

Metre: 7 7 7 7 D
Suggested tunes: *St Edmund; Salzburg*

Bible Sunday

Year A

Nehemiah 8:1-4a (5-6) 8-12
Psalm 119:9-16
Colossians 3:12-17
Matthew 24:30-35

The ears of all the people were attentive to the book of the law. (Nehemiah 8:3b)

Prayer

Gracious God,
you have spoken through the Law and Prophets,
through words of wisdom, history and the psalms,
through the testimony of Evangelists and Apostles
to Jesus Christ,
and above all through the Word made flesh.
We praise you that we can turn to the Bible
whenever we wish to
and read it freely in our own tongue.
We can read new translations that help bring the
age-old message to life,
and we have access to all kinds of resources
designed to deepen our understanding of what
we read.
Forgive us that all too often we leave your word
sitting on a shelf,
unopened,
unexplored.
Help us to recognise the priceless treasure you
have given us in the Scriptures,
and teach us, in the clamour of each day,
to make time to read them, reverently and
thoughtfully,
so that your voice may speak again,
offering light to our path and the way to life in all
its fullness.
Amen.

Nick Fawcett

Psalm 119b

I delight in your decrees, Lord,
everything you say;
gladly will I hear and follow –
never let me stray.
As I ponder your commandments,
guide me in your living way.

All my hope is in your promise,
firm through ages long;
when I suffer, needing comfort,
your word makes me strong.
Those who spurn the truth may taunt me –
still your precepts are my song.

Founded by your timeless statues,
earth and heaven endure;
by those selfsame laws you saved me,
making me secure:
how I love your precious judgements!
I will serve you evermore!

Martin E. Leckebusch

Metre: 85 85 87
Suggested tune: *Angel voices*

Bible Sunday

Year B

Isaiah 55:1-11
Psalm 19:7-14
2 Timothy 3:14 – 4:5
John 5:36b-47

The ordinances of the Lord are true and righteous altogether. (Psalm 19:9b)

Prayer

Gracious God,
we praise you for the way your word has spoken
to so many across the years,
offering a lamp for their path and a faith to live by.
We thank you for the way it has spoken to us,
stirring our imagination,
kindling and nurturing faith,
confronting and questioning,
yet also renewing and uplifting,
each day assuring us of your constant love and
gracious purpose.
Teach us to study your word,
to reflect on its meaning,
and to seek enlightenment,
so that we may hear your voice and respond.
Open our hearts and minds to what you would
say to us,
and help us to listen.
In Jesus' name we pray.
Amen.

Nick Fawcett

Poem

(The reader should hold a large black Bible.)

I do not love this book because it is
black enough to please Puritans,
holy enough to scare demons,
thick enough to stop bullets,
heavy enough to splash flies;
but because sometimes when I read it
I am moved
deeper than tears.

I do not love this book because
they say it is the very words of God,
and polish every dot and comma,
like golden ornaments
in an idolatrous temple;
but because sometimes when I read it
God speaks in a strange tongue
deeper than words.

I do not love this book because
the passionate preacher
beats the truth out of it
with his blunt fist
and sharp ideas,
(for some use the book
to support their opinions,
as others might use it
to support their tables).

But I do love this book
because sometimes when I read it
I am disturbed by a truth
deeper than thought.

And when I read of Jesus,
then I know,
that he is the Truth,
the living Word of God,
whose Spirit moves my soul.

Peter Dainty

Bible Sunday

Year C

Isaiah 45:22-25
Psalm 119:129-136
Romans 15:1-6
Luke 4:16-24

The unfolding of your words gives light. (Psalm 119:130a)

Prayer

O Lord, you have given us your word for a light to shine upon our path; inspire us to meditate on that word and to follow its teaching, that we may find in it the light that shines more and more until the perfect day; through Jesus Christ our Lord.

St Jerome

Psalm 119a

Here is the route laid out for us to follow:
your word reveals the path we ought to tread.
You teach us how to walk and run in freedom
when by the truth we let ourselves be led –
so now we pledge to turn our backs on falsehood,
and to be guided by your law instead.

Here is the spring which offers real refreshment
to weary hearts, worn down by endless strain:
within your word we find such inspiration,
and ample strength to bear our deepest pain.
Lord, in our lives renew your gracious promise
and speak the word which makes us strong again.

Here is the lamp by whose illumination
your holy ways lie open to our sight;
here are the keys of knowledge and discernment:
through your commands you show us what is right;
so, Lord, behind the searching beam of Scripture
we look for you, the source of perfect light.

Martin E. Leckebusch

Metre: 11 10 11 10 11 10
Suggested tune: *Finlandia*

All Saints' Day

Year A

Revelation 7:9-17
Psalm 34:1-10
1 John 3:1-3
Matthew 5:1-12

Salvation belongs to our God who is seated on the throne, and to the Lamb!
(Revelation 7:10)

Prayer

Blessed are you, Lord our God,
for you have called us to share
in the blessedness of your saints.
Grant that in the darkness that is around us
we may be guided by their example
and so serve you in love and peace.
Blessed are you, Father, Son and Holy Spirit.

Rejoicing in the fellowship of all the saints
we pray to the Lord:

Lord, make us to be numbered with your saints
in your eternal glory.
Amen.

David Adam

Poem

There is a famous hostel,
where pilgrims reach their goal,
and standing there to greet them
with towel and with bowl
is Christ the mighty traveller,
the saviour of their race,
who pioneered their pathway
and prepared for them a place.

He kneels and pours the water
on those weary pilgrims' feet,
to cleanse the dust of ages
and to cool the angry heat
of the bruises and the bleeding,
and to wash away the grime
that they've picked up on their journey
through the world of space and time.

So he welcomes them to heaven,
as he welcomed them on earth,
with the gift of living water,
holy sign of their new birth.
And he brings them to the table
where the heavenly feast is spread,
and he pours out wine for gladness
and for love he breaks the bread.
They no longer need the miracle
of body and of blood,
for their Host is ever present
and their souls' sufficient food.

And they do not talk of trial
or betrayal or arrest;
there's no mention of denial,
even by the meanest guest.
For their sins are all forgiven,
none goes out into the night,
as they make a full communion
in the Lord's eternal light.

So he feeds them in the heavens,
as he fed them on the earth,
with the holy bread of mercy
and the wine of holy mirth.

Peter Dainty

All Saints' Day

Year B

Wisdom 3:1-9
or Isaiah 25:6-9
Psalm 24:1-6
Revelation 21:1-6a
John 11:32-44

I saw the holy city, the new Jerusalem, coming down out of heaven from God.
(Revelation 21:2a)

Prayer

Blessed are you, Lord our God,
for you have called us out of darkness
into your own most marvellous light.
Grant that our lives may help to reveal
your love and glory in the world.
As you have called each of us to be saints
may we be worthy of our calling.
Blessed be Father, Son and Holy Spirit.

Amen. *David Adam*

Poem

What a surprise to find –
after believing for years
that heaven was like a garden,
a green and fruitful paradise
of peace and beauty,
or like a palmy South Sea island
lapped by deep blue waters
on a beach of silver sand –
what a surprise to find,
that when, at the end of the Bible,
a piece of heaven
comes floating down to earth,
it isn't a garden at all,
but a City.

And with its gates of pearl
and its streets of gold
it seems not unlike
Las Vegas;
except for its size.
It is a giant cube,
one thousand five hundred miles square,
and one thousand five hundred miles high.
It would seem to be
a planning error
of enormous proportions.

This *Holy City*, as it's called
(surely a contradiction in terms),
has brought heaven
down to earth
with a bump.

But should we be so surprised?
Does God really want us
to dream our destiny away
in a soporific garden,
(or on a pacific beach)
where nothing happens
for all eternity?
For our idea of heaven
often seems to be
a place of self-indulgence,
and of never-ending pleasure.
But in cities
we have to learn how to live
with other people,
in an environment
that's rarely still,
and where there is always
something worthwhile
to do.
For every one of our cities
(even Las Vegas)
is some kind of botched attempt
at civilisation,
and this vision
of the Holy City
is God's way of saying
that he wants civilisation too.

Gardens are wonderful
in their place,
but what better place for a garden
than in a Holy City?

Peter Dainty

All Saints' Day

Year C

Daniel 7:1-3, 15-18
Psalm 149
Ephesians 1:11-23
Luke 6:20-31

I pray that . . . you may know what is the hope to which he has called you, what are the riches of his glorious inheritance among the saints. (Ephesians 1:18)

Prayer

Blessed are you, Lord our God,
for in you and your love we share with the saints in glory.
For all the saints who have gone before us
and revealed your love,
for those in weakness who have revealed your power,
for those who challenge us by their deeds,
we give you thanks and praise.
Blessed are you, Father, Son and Holy Spirit.

We give thanks for all who have built up your Church
through their holiness, their witness and their faith in you.
We give thanks for those who have inspired us
and challenged our way of life.
Lord, grant us the power to be the people you want us to be
and to do what you want us to do.
Bless all who minister to us and teach us your holy word.
We pray for all who are being prepared
for baptism, confirmation, marriage or ordination.

Lord, make us to be numbered with your saints
in that glory which is everlasting.
Amen.

David Adam

Poem

One day the world will live in peace,
for God will settle our disputes
and we shall beat our swords to ploughs
and turn our spears to pruning hooks;
for nation will no longer fight
with nation, and will learn no more
the cruel strategies of war,
but everyone will live secure
and free from fear –
one day.

One day the earth will be renewed,
and harmony will reign
among all living things;
and wolf and leopard, lamb and goat
shall live in peace,
while children play
and meet no harm
from deadly snake
or roaring lion;
for none shall hurt
and none destroy
in all the land;
and as the waters fill the sea
so shall the knowledge
of the Lord our God
fill all the earth –
one day.

One day all those who live and work
like slaves
shall be set free,
debts cancelled,
land restored,
in that great triumph of the Lord,
the year of Jubilee,
when there's an end of death
and grief and pain
when every tear is wiped away –
one day.

Let us then play our part
by getting ready for that day
with all our heart –
today.

Peter Dainty

Fourth Sunday before Advent

Year A

Micah 3:5-12
Psalm 43
  or Psalm 107:1-8
1 Thessalonians 2:9-13
Matthew 24:1-14

Anyone who endures to the end will be saved. (Matthew 24:13)

Prayer

We thank you, Lord,
that in a world of shadows and suffering,
a world wounded by terror and threatened by war
the stars still shine in the night,
and the sun still rises in the morning.

Teach us in the midst of fear and anxiety
to go about our daily duties in peace,
and to value love and goodness where we find
  them.

Help us in days of pain and sorrow
to reach out with comfort and compassion
to those who cry.

Lord, in your mercy: **hear our prayer**.

We pray for all who grieve,
especially those who have lost their loved ones
in any form of human conflict or disaster –
in acts of terror, in situations of poverty and famine,
or through callous crimes –
and also we pray for those who have cared for
  their loved ones in sickness
and must now let them go.
Lord give them all your light and peace.

Lord, in your mercy: **hear our prayer**.

Show us that even in the most hopeless situation
there is still meaning in caring for your precious
  creation
and cherishing the light of beauty in the world;
in nurturing the young
and protecting the weak.

Be with us all when the way is uncertain
so that we may walk with steady footsteps
on the pathway of integrity and truth.

We pray for all those who have power and
  influence in the world – in politics and through
  the media, in business and commerce.
Give them the wisdom and patience to choose the
  things that make for justice and peace.

Lord, in your mercy: **hear our prayer**.

In a world of change,
we thank you for those things which stand for ever.
In the face of all hatred, anger and evil –
we believe that faith, hope and love abide,
these three,
and the greatest of them is love.
Keep us always faithful to the Way of Jesus Christ,
  so that, though human kingdoms fail,
his Kingdom of love may grow for ever. Amen.

Peter Dainty

Poem

The tall, tall candle
has burned down at last.
Now just a scrap of flame
floats in a tiny, shrinking
pool of wax.
The bit of flax
that was wick
has disappeared.
We can remember
when he lighted up our lives,
burned strong and bright.
Now all his shining strength
lies sputtering low,
barely alive,
but not yet altogether out;
not quite.

Elizabeth Rooney

Fourth Sunday before Advent

Year B

Deuteronomy 6:1-9
Psalm 119:1-8
Hebrews 9:11-14
Mark 12:28-34

You shall love the Lord your God with all your heart, and with all your soul, and with all your mind, and with all your strength. (Mark 12:30)

Prayer

Sovereign God,
remind us again today of what really matters to you,
what alone breathes life into worship and service,
all else being as nothing without it –
the gift of love.
Teach us that around this greatest of attributes
revolve the two greatest commandments –
to love you
and others –
and so, we pray, put *your* love within us,
so that it may underlie all we offer now
and do always.
Fill our lives to overflowing,
so that we will truly love you
with all our heart, understanding and strength,
and love our neighbour as ourselves,
through Jesus Christ our Lord.
Amen.

Nick Fawcett

Poem

You have won me with a love
far surpassing mere emotion –
let my heart be yours alone,
overflowing with devotion.

For you hold me in a bond
neither earth nor hell can sever:
in my soul there shines a light
which I know will blaze for ever.

Let your splendour fill my thoughts,
capture my imagination,
till my mind, with pure delight,
turns to you in adoration.

All the strength which I possess,
may I spend it for your pleasure:
every sinew, muscle, nerve,
every skill be yours to treasure.

Nothing else can satisfy
like the joys which I discover
when I give my all to you,
gracious God, eternal Lover.

Martin E. Leckebusch

Fourth Sunday before Advent

Year C

Isaiah 1:10-18
Psalm 32:1-8
2 Thessalonians 1:1-12
Luke 19:1-10

Zacchaeus, hurry and come down; for I must stay at your house today. (Luke 19:5)

Prayer

Lord Jesus Christ,
give us today true eagerness
and genuine determination
to see and hear you for ourselves.
Give us honesty and humility when we hear your call
to admit our faults and be truly sorry;
to welcome you into our lives
and do what we can to make amends,
not to earn your favour
but to demonstrate our gratitude for all you have done,
and our desire to offer you faithful service in return.
Draw near,
meet us,
and work afresh in our lives,
to your glory.
Amen.

Nick Fawcett

Psalm 32

The thrill of God's forgiveness
is more than words can tell –
a peace that comes from pardon,
a sense that all is well:
for those who treat their failures
with candour, not deceit,
will find in God's acceptance
their joy is made complete.

How often we are silent
where sin should be confessed:
we quash the Spirit's prompting
and rob our souls of rest;
but when our lips acknowledge
the wrongs that we have done,
our peace is reinstated,
our guilty load is gone.

Let all whose deepest yearnings
are shown by godly lives
draw daily on God's mercy
until the Day arrives:
for in that final judgement
which settles right and wrong
the Lord will be our refuge,
his saving power, our song.

Lord, may we not be stubborn,
or slow to understand
your Spirit's patient counsel,
your steady guiding hand;
however life may treat us,
your love will bring us through –
with all who know your mercy
we will rejoice in you.

Martin E. Leckebusch

Metre: 76 76 D
Suggested tune: *Thornbury*

Third Sunday before Advent

Year A

Wisdom of Solomon 6:12-16
or Amos 5:18-24
Canticle: Wisdom of Solomon 6:17-20
or Psalm 70
1 Thessalonians 4:13-18
Matthew 25:1-13

Keep awake, for you know neither the day nor the hour. (Matthew 25:13)

Prayer

Lord Jesus Christ,
prepare our hearts to meet you in this time of worship
and when you return in glory
to establish your kingdom.
Confront, instruct and enable us by your Spirit,
so that we will be awake and alert,
equipped to live each moment
as though the day of your coming has dawned,
and ready to welcome you whenever it might be.
Amen.

Nick Fawcett

Poem

Are you ready for the hour of the Kingdom,
when the heirs of God are given their freedom,
and the Lord acclaims those sisters and brothers,
who have spent themselves in service of others?
For the Lord will wipe away all tears from their eyes,
and banish all sorrow and pain and sighs,
and even death will perish in the victory of life
when the Kingdom of God is come.

And at midnight, when the voice of the bridegroom
wakes us from our sleep to share in the banquet,
will your lamp of faith be empty and smoking
and the Lord of life say, 'I never knew you'?
For the new world's door will be open wide
to receive those who stand by their neighbours' side
with their lamps burning brightly till the night gives way
to the dawn of the Day of God.

Peter Dainty

Third Sunday before Advent

Year B

Jonah 3:1-5,10
Psalm 62:5-12
Hebrews 9:24-28
Mark 1:14-20

Follow me and I will make you fish for people. (Mark 1:17)

Prayer

Lord Jesus Christ,
help us today to hear again your call to discipleship,
and to follow faithfully wherever you would lead.
May the good news of your living, dying and
rising among us
resonate afresh deep within,
stirring us to sincere repentance,
deeper faith
and renewed service.
Teach us now to live more authentically as your
people,
in the light of your kingdom.
Amen.

Nick Fawcett

Poem

We were sitting by the seashore
mending our nets,
just to make an honest living
and to pay all our debts,
when a voice from the blue
woke us from our reverie:
'Leave your nets where they are, boys,
and come and follow me.'

'And I will make you to become
real fishermen for me.'

And when people heard him preaching
the word of the Lord,
they were crowding by the lakeside
where our vessels were moored.
Jesus gave us a shout
as he took off his coat:
'It would help me a lot, boys,
if I could use your boat.'

'And I will make you to become
real fishermen for me.'

We had spent the long night fishing
far out on the deep,
and we hadn't caught a thing
and were ready for sleep.
But the Lord turned us back,
saying: 'Boys, just try again.'
And the catch was so great, we
could hardly drag it in.

'And I will make you to become
real fishermen for me.'

We were making heavy weather
caught out in a storm,
clinging fast to the rigging,
praying hard for the dawn;
when the Master appeared,
walking calmly on the waves,
calling: 'Don't you believe, boys,
that God's the one who saves?'

'And I will make you to become
real fishermen for me.'

We were sailing with the master
asleep in the stern,
when the sky grew black and stormy
and the wind took a turn.
But the Master arose,
when he heard of our alarm,
and the power of his word made
the wind and waters calm.

'And I will make you to become
real fishermen for me.'

Peter Dainty

Third Sunday before Advent

Year C

Job 19:23-27a
Psalm 17:1-9
2 Thessalonians 2:1-5, 13-17
Luke 20:27-38

In my flesh I shall see God. (Job 19:26b)

Prayer

Bring us, O Lord God, at our last awakening
into the house and gate of heaven,
to enter into that gate and dwell in that house,
where there shall be no darkness nor dazzling, but
one equal light;
no noise nor silence, but one equal music;
no fears nor hopes, but one equal possession;
no ends nor beginnings, but one equal eternity;
in the habitations of thy glory and dominion
world without end.

John Donne

Hymn

The changing of the seasons,
the passing of the years,
remind us just how swiftly
a lifetime disappears;
our frailty holds us captive –
we grow, and age, and die –
yet you remain for ever,
eternal Lord most high.

We find that we inhabit
a world of constant change:
our parents' views and lifestyles
our children find so strange.
Let every generation
its futile dreams pursue!
Lord, you alone are changeless –
our trust we place in you.

We gather to remember
a course that has been run,
a journey now completed,
a battle fought and won.
Be near us, Lord, in mercy,
sustain us while we grieve;
our hope is life eternal –
your promise we believe.

You strengthen and direct us,
our true and faithful guide;
we turn to you for refuge;
our courage you provide.
Through Jesus you have shown us
how much you love our race –
so keep us, heavenly Father,
forever in your grace.

Martin E. Leckebusch

Metre: 7 6 7 6 D
Suggested tune: *Thornbury*

Second Sunday before Advent

Year A

Zephaniah 1:7, 12-18
Psalm 90:1-8 (9-11) 12
1 Thessalonians 5:1-11
Matthew 25:14-30

Those who have, more will be given, and they will have an abundance;
but from those who have nothing, even what they have will be taken away.
(Matthew 25:29)

Prayer

Blessed are you, Lord our God,
for you have given us all talents and abilities.
You have created each of us in a unique way,
that we may give our own unique service and
talents to you.
Blessed are you, Father, Son and Holy Spirit.

Lord, giver of all good gifts,
we give you thanks for all you have given us.
May we share our talents and use them
to the benefit of others and for your glory.
We pray today for all who tell others of your love
and proclaim the Gospel.
We ask your blessing upon all who minister to
others.

Giver of all good gifts,
hear us and help us to live to your glory.
Amen.

David Adam

Poem

(This could possibly be for three readers.)

And the first question is this –
When the king returns
and asks for an account of our stewardship,
will there be anyone left
with even a single talent in their hand,
who can step forward and say:
'I still have what you first gave me;
not increased, to be sure,
but certainly not diminished;
take it back again'?
Or will the problem be
to find any talents at all,
buried beneath the ashes
of a wasted world?

And the second question is this –
Will the king cast his worthless servants
into the outer darkness,
where there is weeping and wailing
and gnashing of teeth?
Or will he consider it juster punishment
to leave us in the darkness
we have made for ourselves;
and go in search of another world
to try again?

And the third question is this –
What are we going to do
to avoid the other two questions?

Peter Dainty

Second Sunday before Advent

Year B

Daniel 12:1-3
Psalm 16
Hebrews 10:11-14 (15-18) 19-25
Mark 13:1-8

At that time Michael, the great prince, the protector of your people, shall arise.
(Daniel 12:1)

Prayer

Lord Jesus Christ,
we look to you for wisdom and discernment,
strength and support,
guidance and inspiration.
Reveal to us, as we worship you,
more of your sovereign purpose and gracious will,
through working for it now,
trusting in your love despite all that fights
against it,
confident that in the fullness of time,
you will come again to reign here on earth,
as you do in heaven.
Equip us, then, to stand firm,
and, in a world of turmoil and strife,
to keep faith that, though all else may fail,
you will not.
Amen.

Nick Fawcett

Poem

If you ever get to heaven,
you'll be shown around
by a guardian angel.
And one of the places you'll visit
on the very first day
will be the Celestial Bank.
(I know there is a bank,
because Jesus told us
to lay up treasures for ourselves
in heaven.)
So they'll bring out your account,
and with a frown and a sigh
and a shaking of the head
they'll probably say,
'If only you'd put more in
on earth,
you could have taken more out
in heaven.'

So be warned –
it isn't yet too late
to start investing.

Peter Dainty

Second Sunday before Advent

Year C

Malachi 4:1-2a
Psalm 98
2 Thessalonians 3:6-13
Luke 21:5-19

See, the day is coming, burning like an oven, when all the arrogant and all evildoers will be stubble. (Malachi 4:1a)

Prayer

Living God,
teach us to trust in your future
and to keep faith in the final dawning of your
kingdom,
but save us from dwelling on such things,
indulging in futile speculation
or being taken in by the conjectures of others.
Teach us, rather, to live faithfully for you,
serving and honouring you
through following the way of Christ
despite every pressure to deflect us from it.
Help us to consecrate the present to you,
and to leave all else in your hands,
through Jesus Christ our Lord.
Amen.

Nick Fawcett

Poem

How good it is to give you thanks:
we honour you, our mighty King!
Your endless love, your constant care
inspire the praise we gladly bring
in word and music, day and night:
to worship you is our delight.

How glad you make us by your deeds!
Your thoughts are deep, beyond compare!
The greatness of your wonders, Lord,
it is our pleasure to declare;
to those who place their trust in you
your glory shines through all you do.

How many fail to grasp the truth,
or hear your voice but turn away;
they flourish now, but disregard
the prospect of a judgement day
when righteousness and mercy meet
and signal evil's full defeat.

And yet how gracious is your call,
for you address us now as friends
and guide our lives on fruitful paths
until, at length, our journey ends:
Lord God, how matchless are your ways!
How right it is to sing your praise!

Martin E. Leckebusch

Metre: 8 8 8 8 88
Suggested tune: *Melita*

Christ the King

Year A

Ezekiel 34:11-16, 20-24
Psalm 95: 1-7
Ephesians 1:15-23
Matthew 25:31-46

I will seek out my sheep. (Ezekiel 34:12)

Prayer

Lord Jesus Christ,
humble yet exalted,
servant yet sovereign,
teach us afresh today that through honouring others
we honour you,
and through serving them we serve you.
Awaken us to your presence all around us
and to your call, especially in the cry of the needy,
and in responding to the hungry,
the sick,
the lonely
and the oppressed,
may we respond also to you.
Reach out to us in mercy,
that we might reach out to you and to them in love.
Amen.

Nick Fawcett

Hymn

Jesus stands among the children
smeared with others' guilt at birth –
haunted by unspoken questions,
made to feel devoid of worth.
Refugees from threat or danger,
far from home through troubled years:
Jesus senses all their turmoil –
parents' anguish, children's fears.

Jesus stands with those rejected
by their nearest flesh and blood,
feeling sorrow with the lonely,
shunned, and seldom understood.
Jesus walks among the homeless,
where the street becomes a bed –
finding, far from heaven's splendour,
nowhere else to lay his head.

Jesus stands where justice falters,
where the truth is bought and sold:
well he knows the bitter poison
of a trust betrayed for gold.
Lies and groundless accusations;
torture dealt by callous hands;
execution, slow and painful –
each of these he understands.

Jesus bids us stand beside him –
Man of sorrows, Lord of all! –
as with wounded hands he offers
grace and strength to those who fall.
He transforms our path of suffering,
brings us newness by his pain;
in the help we give to others
we begin to share his reign.

Martin E. Leckebusch

Metre: 8 7 8 7 D
Suggested tune: *Blaenwern*

Christ the King

Year B

Daniel 7:9, 10, 13, 14
Psalm 93
Revelation 1:4b-8
John 18:33-37

I saw one like a human being coming with the clouds of heaven. (Daniel 7:13a)

Prayer

Lord Jesus Christ,
despised,
rejected,
yet risen and enthroned on high,
reign in our hearts and rule in our lives.
Grant that, just as we extol you now –
singing your praises,
giving you glory
and declaring our commitment,
so we may similarly acclaim you always –
praising, glorifying and serving you
through obedience to your will,
in thought, word and deed.
In your name we ask it.
Amen.

Nick Fawcett

Poem

They sometimes say that Jesus was a King,
and yet he had no throne or golden crown,
no royal robes or jewelled ring.
He had no army to enforce his Law;
his wealth was not in palaces or lands;
he lived his life among the poor.

But King he is; and though he reigns unseen,
and love's the only power at his command –
in truth, no greater King has ever been,
whose love and peace shall rule in every land.

Peter Dainty

Christ the King

Year C

Jeremiah 23:1-6
Psalm 46
Colossians 1:11-20
Luke 23:33-43

He himself is before all things, and in him all things hold together.
(Colossians 1:17)

Prayer

Blessed are you, Lord our God,
for you love us with an everlasting love
and sent your Son to be our Saviour.
He came and died that we might live.
Now he is the King of kings and Lord of lords.
May we do your will and share in your kingdom.
Blessed are you, Father, Son and Holy Spirit.

Father, we give you thanks
that in Christ Jesus you have redeemed the world.
He died that we might live.
He reigns with you and seeks us to be part of his kingdom.
We pray for all who are seeking to serve you in their daily lives.
We remember especially
any who are being persecuted for their faith.
Lord, give us the courage to speak for you
and to witness to your love.

Lord, your kingdom come
in us as in heaven.
Amen.

David Adam

Poem

(*For up to five readers.*)

Three cheers for Jesus!
He comes to be our King.
He'll overthrow the tyrants,
and wealth and freedom bring.
He'll outlaw every evil –
all pain and fear and greed.
He'll take over the government
and meet our every need.

Two cheers for Jesus.
He claims to be our King,
but he's striding through the Temple
and upsetting everything.
He's scattering our profits
and the businesses we've made;
is he really fit to rule us
if he spoils our holy trade?

One cheer for Jesus.
He came to be our King,
but now he stands on trial,
red with the whip's sharp sting.
With crown of thorns they mock him,
scorned by official power.
He's helpless with authority;
this cannot be his hour.

No cheers for Jesus.
He's surely not our King.
They've nailed him to a wooden cross
while people laugh and sing.
The one we thought would save us
they curse and wound and kill.
Our hopes and expectations
die with him on that hill.

Now heaven cheers for Jesus.
The world has had its say;
and God has raised him from the dead –
there dawns another day.
Disciples stand bewildered
beside an empty grave,
but soon they will be cheering too
the Christ who came to save.

Peter Dainty